PT 2178
Schweitzer, Albert, 1875-1965.
Goethe; four studies

DATE	ISSUED TO

PT 2178
Schweitzer, Albert, 1875-1965.
Goethe; four studies

GOETHE

FOUR STUDIES
BY
ALBERT SCHWEITZER

THE BEACON PRESS

SCHWEITZER SERIES

The Africa of Albert Schweitzer, by Charles R. Joy and Melvin Arnold (published with Harper and Brothers)

Albert Schweitzer: An Anthology, edited by Charles R. Joy (published with Harper and Brothers)

Albert Schweitzer: Life and Message, by Magnus Ratter

Albert Schweitzer: A Vindication, by George Seaver

The Animal World of Albert Schweitzer, edited by Charles R. Joy, drawings by Richard F. Bartlett, photographs by Charles R. Joy

Goethe: Four Studies by Albert Schweitzer, edited by Charles R. Joy

Indian Thought and Its Development, translated by Mrs. Charles E. B. Russell

Music in the Life of Albert Schweitzer, edited by Charles R. Joy (published with Harper and Brothers)

Path to Reconstruction: A Brief Introduction to Schweitzer's Philosophy of Civilization, by Mrs. Charles E. B. Russell

The Psychiatric Study of Jesus, translated by Charles R. Joy

The Wit and Wisdom of Albert Schweitzer, edited by Charles R. Joy

Goethe

FOUR STUDIES
BY
ALBERT SCHWEITZER

Translated, with an introduction, by
CHARLES R. JOY

THE BEACON PRESS · BOSTON

turn

First Edition, *Goethe: Two Addresses*

Copyright, 1948

Enlarged Bicentennial Edition, *Goethe: Four Studies*

Copyright, 1949

THE BEACON PRESS

All rights reserved

TO

EMMY MARTIN

The grace of the Munster Valley
is yours as well

The fires of mercy which you feed
burn within you

PREFATORY NOTE

This book, prepared for the two hundredth anniversary of the birth of Johann Wolfgang von Goethe, consists of three addresses delivered by Albert Schweitzer, as well as an article written by him for the magazine *Europe*.

The first of the four, chronologically, was the address given on August 28, 1928, when Frankfort bestowed the Goethe Prize on Dr. Schweitzer at the Goethe House in that city. The address was taken down in shorthand, and first printed in the Yearbook of the Free German Academy, Frankfort on the Main, 1928. It was later translated into English by Mr. C. T. Campion, published in *The Hibbert Journal,* circulated in America in a paper-bound leaflet, and included in *Goethe: Two Addresses* (Beacon Press, 1948). In that form, the first portion of the address was omitted. In the present edition, the address appears in its complete form and in a fresh translation.

The second, chronologically, was given on March 22, 1932, at the University of Frankfort, on the one hundredth anniversary of Goethe's death. It was issued by the C. H. Beck Publishing House in Munich; the first publication in English was that of the Beacon Press in *Goethe: Two Addresses.*

The third was an article contributed by Dr. Schweitzer to the French magazine *Europe,* which issued on April 15, 1932, a special number dedicated to Goethe on the hundredth anniversary of his death (Vol. XXVIII, No. 112). It is here translated for the first time from French into English, with the gracious permission of the publishers of *Europe.*

The fourth was an address given on July 9, 1932, at Ulm, in Germany, and is here translated directly from the manuscript, with Dr. Schweitzer's kind consent.

7

The order in which these chapters appear is the chrono-
logical order, with one exception. It seems fitting that the
longer, more general and more adequate studies of Goethe's
life, character, literary genius and thought should precede
the shorter Goethe Prize Address, in which Schweitzer acknowledges his own indebtedness to Goethe.

Since all of these studies were prepared for different audi-
ences, some repetition will be found. Such duplication has
been permitted to stand, for each of these chapters is a unity
and each is a valuable contribution to the subject. In the
translation of Goethe's poetry, the meter and rhyme schemes
of the original have been preserved. This will account for
some slight variance in meaning between the German text
and the English version.

These studies are important as a contribution to our understanding of both Goethe and Schweitzer. The surprising
similarity in the lives and foundation principles of these two
great men, living a century apart, is set forth in the Introduction, and will, I think, be clearly evident in the studies
themselves.

—CHARLES R. JOY

Newton Highlands
Massachusetts
1949

ACKNOWLEDGMENT

Grateful acknowledgment is made to Henry Holt and Company, Inc., N.Y., for permission to reprint copyrighted material from *Out of My Life and Thought* by Albert Schweitzer.

CONTENTS

INTRODUCTION

GOETHE AND SCHWEITZER: PARALLEL LIVES

"No one can write his real religious life with pen or pencil. It is written only in actions, and its seal is our own character, not our orthodoxy." This is Dr. Wilfred Thomason Grenfell speaking. He and Albert Schweitzer are kindred souls. One devoted his life to the fishermen of the frozen north, and the other to the natives of the equatorial jungle, but the same glowing motivation lies at the core of their hearts. "Whether we, our neighbor, or God is the judge," Grenfell continues, "absolutely the only value of our 'religious' life to ourselves or to anyone is what it fits us for and enables us to do. Creeds, when expressed only in words, clothes, or abnormal lives, are daily growing less acceptable as passports to Paradise. What my particular intellect can accept cannot commend me to God. His 'well done' is only spoken to the man who 'wills to do His will.' "

The world has an insatiable curiosity (or is it an abiding concern?) to know the reasons which lead men to forsake comfort and affluence and prestige to found hospitals at St. Anthony in Labrador or at Lambarene on the banks of the Ogowe River. It is not easy for the ordinary man to understand. The children of St. Francis have always been considered a bit mad by their contemporaries. It is much easier to comprehend the rich young man of the parable who went away sorrowing because he could not give up his privileged position to take the hard road of discipleship.

Albert Schweitzer has explained the reasons why he left his important teaching post, his writings in theology and philosophy, the great libraries and old organs of Europe, to

13

study medicine and bury himself in the steaming tropics of Africa. He went because he had no right to happiness while other men suffered, he went to repay a debt which the white races owed to the black, he went because he felt he must make some return for the privileges of his lot, he went because he had to give satisfying expression to the supreme ethics of his life: love in selfless service.

There is something pure and lifted-up about all this, like the holy grail in the Arthurian legends, and if we do not wholly understand, still we do not strive with stained and sullied hands to lift the crimson samite from the golden chalice. There are quiet reserves in the lives of all great men which must be respected. Only when they themselves bid us penetrate into the inner sanctuaries of the soul may we enter.

In these studies of Goethe, Albert Schweitzer reveals more frankly than in any other place some of the influences which molded his character. He whom we are beginning to reverence as one of the rare spiritual leaders of all time humbly acknowledges a debt which is hardly hinted at elsewhere in his writings. He whom we call a master calls himself a disciple, a disciple to the great immortal of German literature, Johann Wolfgang von Goethe.

I may be permitted to quote from a personal letter to me, written since the appearance of the first edition of this book, in which Dr. Schweitzer says:

Goethe is the personality with which I have been most deeply concerned. St. Paul, who, I think, has had a decisive influence upon me, belongs to an epoch too far away and too different from our own. The details of his life are too little known for me to converse with him and commune with him, as I can with Goethe, who seems to me so alive even in the contradictory facts, autobiographical and quasi-autobiographical, that we possess about him. What attracts me in him is that he is a man of action at the same time that he is a poet, a thinker, and in certain domains a savant and a man of research. And what binds us together in the deepest depths of our beings is his philosophy of nature.

As one of the endearing traits of Schweitzer's character is his profound and sterling humility, it is indeed possible that he overrates the influence of Goethe upon his life. Certainly he does not recognize, or at least he does not underline, the many flaws in Goethe's nature. We who can see both men with some perspective, though one is long dead and the other throbbingly alive, quickly perceive that in moral and spiritual sublimity it is Schweitzer who is the cloisterer and Goethe who is the novice.

In the light of Schweitzer's own grateful testimony, however, one may not doubt the worth of the heritage which Goethe handed down to him. One may go farther than Schweitzer and point out, as the following pages will attempt to point out, the many striking similarities between the lives of these two men. One may even venture to suggest that Goethe's contribution to Schweitzer's life and thought was greater than Schweitzer himself is aware of. But after one has so daringly ventured, he must inevitably revert to the simple conviction that Schweitzer is a man in his own right, and that on the edge of the primeval forest he has blazed trails through the ethical wilderness of modern life, which may some day be the traveled highways of a better humanity. He is no colorless follower. He himself is a pioneer.

While it is not, therefore, quite true to say that in these studies of Goethe, Schweitzer is writing his own autobiography, it is nonetheless true that in these studies one of the missing keys to the understanding of his life is presented. It is when we bring Goethe and Schweitzer face to face that comprehension begins.

With touching humility Schweitzer acknowledges his debt to Goethe. First of all, he recognizes in Goethe a man who has remained loyal to a simple nature philosophy in a day when the world and nature were being forced by the philoso-

phers into conformity with man's ideas for the sake of
harmony. This simple nature philosophy was Schweitzer's
also, and while he does not say that he derived his philosophy
from Goethe, he does pay tribute to the man who, before
him, stood guard at a post which most thinkers had de-
serted. Both men were humble in the presence of the
phenomena of nature. We must not try to get behind them,
Goethe constantly insisted. "Man's noblest experience is
that of awe, and if the phenomena as such are awe-inspiring,
let him be content. He will mount no higher; he should
not try to get behind the experience." This, too, was
Schweitzer's position. He thought, perhaps erroneously,
that he was the first Westerner who dared to be absolutely
skeptical with regard to our knowledge of the objective
world, without at the same time renouncing the affirmative
ethical attitude. He believed profoundly that any world
view which was not based on despair of intellectual knowledge must be artificial and fictitious, since it rested on an un-
trustworthy interpretation of the universe.

Goethe, however, was a strange mixture of pagan and
Christian. With his artist friends he copied the paintings
in the wonderful Sistine Chapel in Rome, which was the
coolest place to work in the oppressive heat of August, and
actually dozed in the papal chair. He saw the Pope celebrate
mass at Christmas and Corpus Christi, and then wrote:

I have grown too old a Diogenes to be in any way impressed.
. . . It is stupid to bolster up a delusion with all this fuss and
feathers, and when I look at all these mummeries as an artist
and as a poet I find them wearisome and trivial, however much
they may impress the infantile and sensuous mind.

Schweitzer could never have uttered these words, nor
could he have dozed on the papal throne. He had too much
respect for the faith and convictions of other men. But he,
too, in his inmost thought was impatient with the empty and

traditional forms of religion. One may search his writings in vain for any of the old forms of Christian dogma. His simple faith in the profound principle of Christian love which he finds in Jesus is unmarred by the theological speculations of the later centuries. He is sure that the truth that was in the ethics of Jesus can stand alone. It needs no scaffolding round it, no shoring to stay it. Sectarianism means as little to him as it did to Goethe. Christianity is for him chaotic in its very greatness. It is no longer a force in the world. It could not prevent the war. It is shot through with weakness and mistakes. It needs to be filled again to overflowing with the spirit of Jesus if it is to achieve its destined purpose. Yet Schweitzer believes earnestly that the human soul is capable of asserting itself triumphantly over a universe which is both creative and destructive, good and evil, a universe which offers no evidence that man is its goal or even its major concern.

Schweitzer found inspiration in Goethe's *Harzreise* ("Journey into the Harz Mountains"), when in the winter of 1777 Goethe set out through the worst kind of weather to visit a man who needed his help. Again and again in later years, Schweitzer, called upon to undertake some difficult and unpleasant duty, said to himself, "This is a *Harzreise* for you."

At this point, however, Schweitzer idealizes Goethe. The latter's service to humanity was enormous, in actual accomplishment perhaps more significant than Schweitzer's own contribution, but many times Goethe failed in his relations with individuals, refusing to make the *Harzreise* himself, seeking escape from unpleasant duties, and deliberately shunning those kindly human relations in which Schweitzer has found his highest satisfaction and usefulness.

Dr. Schweitzer himself generously comes to Goethe's defense in a letter to me about these words of mine:

I have the impression that in comparing me with Goethe you unduly favor me over him, and I must take his part. I think I understand him, and therefore I am not inclined to condemn him even when he may seem to merit condemnation. There is a kind of uncertainty and indecisiveness about him in many things, and particularly in critical situations, that is very disappointing. It is a hereditary affliction exactly like a shaking sickness. And I have the impression that he himself was aware of it, and (without admitting it to others) suffered because of it. He was not the artist in life, as people like to represent him, but a man who had a hard time of it through an uncertainty and an indecisiveness that handicapped him. It is quite unfair that I should derive advantage from the fact that I have been carved out of a harder wood. Therefore I do not venture to judge him when he obeys another impulse. Everything comes from that inherited disposition. How grateful must we be for an inherited disposition that keeps us fit, and how carefully we must guard against taking it in any way as merit! So I have an understanding love for Goethe. This is dominant in my feeling for him.

This also impresses me: in spite of his natural tendency, he clung to his purpose of being an active man. And perhaps his scattered activity, just because it was scattered, was more difficult than my unified work. But in this activity his struggle for humanity is revealed. Both of us have this in common: our lives have so developed that the activities we have undertaken have not permitted us to bring our intellectual lifework to an end in composure and leisure. Only by virtue of enormous exertions have we finished a goodly fragment of it. In this we are comrades of fate, and for long years this fact has bound me to him. It is as if he were there to comfort me.

Finally one last thing. Fate planned it well that we did not live in the same age to meet one another and to deal with one another. Had it been otherwise, we should have been kept apart by what in each of us was strange and incomprehensible to the other. We might even have been adversaries. As it is, however, I may examine his personality and his life as a whole, and allow them to influence me, and cultivate an ideal relation with him, with which no reality can interfere. So I get from him the best and the most perfect that one can get from him, that which those who lived with him could not know, just as they who dwell in the mountains do not see the noblest heights in that majesty in which they appear to those who see them in the distance, rising from the foothills, clothed in haze.

There can be no doubt that Schweitzer found great and constant comfort, when the pressure of hospital duties made his music and his writing and even his thinking impossible, in the fact that Goethe also made the same sacrifice, if sacrifice it be. Goethe came to regard it as his destiny to exhaust himself in the daily round of administrative duties, as before he had found expression for his inmost spirit in the exalted moods of literature. Indeed, he came to think of his poetic gifts as a lovely but quite unrelated matter, and to rejoice in the happy fate that had brought him to his government post at Weimar. With complete devotion and with unremitting zest he entered into the performance of an astonishing variety of duties. He reconstructed the mines at Ilmenau, directed the court theater, he had charge of schools and roads, he built factories and laboratories, tore down a hospital and renovated a castle and strove to introduce economy into the finances of the district. The multitudinous details of his life as they appear in his daily journals are literally astounding. There was nothing too unimportant for him to turn his hand and his mind to.

Occasionally, it is true, the artist in him rebelled. Once he exclaimed: "We poets should be treated as the Dukes of Saxony treated Luther—forbidden to walk the streets, confined in a strong fortress. Would that someone would treat me that way, then my *Tell* would be completed by Michaelmas." At fifty Goethe was director of the court theater and minister of education, but his *Faust* was still unfinished. Then he roused himself, and by extraordinary effort added about eight hundred lines to what he had written years before. So the first part was ready for publication when he was fifty-two, but he did not actually publish it until he was fifty-nine. Even then it appeared only as a fragment and not another line was added until he was seventy-six. The book was not finished until he was eighty-two, the year of his death.

Goethe took immense satisfaction in his administrative responsibilities. Yet, in the midst of a statement to that effect, he wrote: "I feel like a snared bird. I have wings and cannot use them." He praised Marcus Aurelius in that he did not permit his writing to absorb all his energies, and then, as if involuntarily, added:

So far as I can I am diverting the water from the fountains and cascades to the mills and the irrigation ditches; but while I am not looking some wicked sprite turns the tap and the water all runs away in a torrent. I think I am riding on my hack horse to the station where I must go, and suddenly the mare beneath me turns into a glorious, uncontrollable, winged steed, and off she flies with me.

So also has it been with Schweitzer. He, too, has found his literary, musical and philosophical work completely submerged under the practical burdens of administering his hospital. Digging postholes for new buildings, fighting the traveler ants on their destructive inroads, planting a garden hewn out of the jungle, writing in longhand his many letters, keeping the records of the pharmacy, ordering supplies a year ahead, operating on the sick and burying the dead, teaching and preaching to the natives, always under tremendous pressure, with inadequate assistance and meager support, Schweitzer has carried on his enterprise as a symbol of the Christian love he came into the forest to impart and to exemplify. Reconciled as he has been to arduous labor, there have been fleeting moments of regret that he could not continue or complete some important intellectual undertaking. His work on *The Philosophy of Civilization* still lies unfinished. The first two volumes, *The Decay and Restoration of Civilization*, and *Civilization and Ethics*, appeared in 1923. Will he finish it? It would be a desolating disappointment to him if this became impossible, but not until the end of October, 1948, was he able to drop the exhausting work of the hospital and return to Europe with the hope of completing it. In his vision of ministrations of mercy continuing in the primeval forests after he has gone, he finds his consolation, just as Faust found it at the very end of his life in his vision of the green meadows and gardens, the woods and towns which he purposes to wrest from the sea for the benefit of the people.

Schweitzer finds inspiration again in Goethe's devotion to natural science. It is a salutary discipline, he insists, for one who has been dealing with intellectual concepts to face the hard facts of life and the universe. Certainly Goethe neglected the supreme gifts of his genius to study all the sciences that reveal the nature of the world: botany, geology, zoölogy, chemistry, physics, anthropology. As Schweitzer points out, he was regarded by his time as only an amateur in these fields of research, but in reality he was much more than that. At the age of thirty-five Goethe discovered the intermaxillary bone in the human cheek, which up to that time had been found only in animals. Science jeered at his conclusion that we could not discern the difference between the brute and the man, only a century afterwards to acclaim it as a great discovery. It was Goethe who glimpsed the Darwinian theory seventy years before Darwin, and proclaimed that every bone was a part or fragment of the vertebral system. Of course, Goethe was sometimes wrong. The theory of light for which he contended valiantly, and sometimes bitterly, until the day of his death was a mistaken theory.

In like manner Schweitzer turned in the full maturity of his early success to the science of medicine, and found it through all the ensuing years a rewarding, if rigorous, regime. He proved to be a capable practitioner in the field of tropical medicine, and all that he learned and experienced enhanced the spiritual richness of his life.

In two other ways Schweitzer credits Goethe for strong influence upon his life. Goethe had an abiding concern for justice, and in this Schweitzer is one with him. Indeed, Schweitzer's sense of justice far surpasses Goethe's. Goethe's treatment of Friederike was not the sole instance in Goethe's life of gross injustice. When confronted with stern or unpleasant realities Goethe often took refuge in flight; Schweitzer never.

Second, Goethe was a man of his age, trying to share all of its activities and all of its aspirations. Schweitzer is perhaps less a man of his age than Goethe, if for no other reason than that he is so far removed from the main currents of it. Yet, while Goethe comprehended the life of his time in its outward aspects so fully, Schweitzer has penetrated more deeply into the inner spirit of mankind than Goethe ever did. Here it is Schweitzer that is the master.

In one respect both men stand largely aloof from their age. Neither has much respect for the opinions of the multitude. Each has an instinctive disdain for the mob. Neither is moved by the applause or the condemnation of the crowd. Each believes in the individual. In Goethe's letters and journals there is hardly a reference to the mighty disturbances of his time. When the Rhine Confederation was formed, he remarked that a quarrel between servants and cab drivers on a bridge excited him more than the partition of the Holy Roman Empire. Similarly, the stirring events of these recent decades have found little reflection in the writings of Albert Schweitzer. Neither man has been much interested in the external pattern of revolution or reform. Goethe wished to partition the great estates for the benefit of the people, but gave up his dream in the end as impossible of achievement, saying: "Meantime one waters his own garden, even though he can not produce rain for the whole country." Schweitzer devotes some attention to the great problems arising from colonization and trade, but has no far-reaching solutions to offer.

Goethe's lip sometimes curled in contempt for men. He quoted with approval Ariosto's comment upon the mob: "They should have been killed at birth." He gave vent to his disillusionment in these words: "We are sure in our younger days that we can build palaces for mankind, but with experience we find that the most we can do is to clean up their dunghills." Schweitzer seldom feels such despair. Once, indeed, in a moment of weariness, he threw himself into a chair in his consulting room and groaned out, "What a blockhead I was to come out here to doctor savages like these!" But with apparent approval he quotes the quiet rebuke of his Negro orderly, "Yes, Doctor, here on earth you are a great blockhead, but not in heaven."

Any student of the lives of these two men must be aware of other similarities between them, which Schweitzer does not refer to. Both men have a deep and clear-sighted devotion to truth, to truth at any cost. Neither is blinded by the conventions and traditional beliefs of the age, or even of the ages. Goethe once said that the discovery of the earth's motion around the sun was the most sublime discovery ever made by the human mind, "more important than the whole Bible put together." Even stronger, then, than his love for beauty, for the exaltation of poetry, was his love for truth. It is not in any religious faith, not in any creative art, that the clue to his character is to be found. It is to be found in his devotion to science. He was not a Christian, unless you agree with his own daring conjecture that perhaps he was the only Christian.

Schweitzer, too, is a fearless seeker for truth, for truth unshackled. "If thought is to set out on its journey unhampered," he said, "it must be prepared for anything, even for arrival at intellectual agnosticism. But even if our will-to-action is destined to wrestle endlessly and unavailingly with an agnostic view of the universe and of life, still this painful disenchantment is better for it than persistent refusal to think out its position at all. For this disenchantment does,

at any rate, mean that we are clear as to what we are doing."
In Schweitzer's studies of Jesus and Paul, and in his em-
phasis upon the central significance of the eschatological
element in their thought, the whole structure of Christian
theology is shaken. Schweitzer himself well knew that his
conclusions would be considered heretical, even blasphe-
mous. He admitted that his views, although they were
reached after much careful and prayerful research, would
not be acceptable to the piety of his day. He makes this
quite clear in *Out of My Life and Thought*, when he writes:

Since the essential nature of the spiritual is truth, every new
truth means ultimately something won. Truth is under all circumstances more valuable than nontruth, and this must apply
to truth in the realm of history as to other kinds of truth. Even
if it comes in a guise which piety finds strange and at first makes
difficulties for her, the final result can never mean injury; it can
only mean greater depth. Religion has, therefore, no reason for
trying to avoid coming to terms with historical truth.

The historical Jesus which Schweitzer uncovered at the
end of his quest was a man of his time, and not of our time;
only as his spirit, which is of no time, but of all time, is re-
born in our hearts can the life and teaching of Jesus be of
inspiration to us. Schweitzer never faltered in his search for
truth. "Buy the truth, and sell it not," advised the writer of
Proverbs. Schweitzer would not sell the truth which he had
bought to win the pottage of praise. It was his precious birth-
right.

Goethe and Schweitzer alike, Christian in no conven-
tional sense of the term, were sure that in the end the truth,
despised, forsworn, disglorified, condemned as impious and
profane, would win the day and set men everlastingly free.

The sure basis of Schweitzer's ethical and religious
thought is his conception of reverence—reverence for life.
In his search for some stable foundation for the palace of
ethics he was building, Schweitzer was long baffled. Then,

one day, on a tedious errand of mercy in the African jungle, he found it. Let Schweitzer describe the experience himself:

Slowly we crept upstream, laboriously feeling—it was the dry season—for the channels between the sandbanks. Lost in thought I sat on the deck of the barge, struggling to find the elementary and universal conception of the ethical which I had not discovered in any philosophy. Sheet after sheet I covered with disconnected sentences, merely to keep myself concentrated on the problem. Late on the third day, at the very moment when, at sunset, we were making our way through a herd of hippopotamuses, there flashed upon my mind, unforeseen and unsought, the phrase, "Reverence for Life." The iron door had yielded: the path in the thicket had become visible. Now I had found my way to the idea in which world- and life-affirmation and ethics are contained side by side! Now I knew that the world-view of ethical world- and life-affirmation, together with its ideals of civilization, is founded in thought.

This was to him an ecstatic experience, a transfiguring mount of vision. This was his peak of Darien, from which he gazed in rapture upon a shining, limitless sea. Is it not strange that Schweitzer was unaware of another presence on that peak, that he did not perceive Goethe standing there beside him? For Goethe, too, had caught a glimpse of this truth. He, too, had had his transfiguration hour.

Schweitzer was very familiar with Goethe's *Wilhelm Meister*. He must have read again and again of Wilhelm's visit to the Pedagogic Province, where he is taking his son Felix. Somehow what Goethe had written and taught must have become so integral a part of Schweitzer's subliminal self that he failed to recognize in the words that came to him on the mount the accents of Goethe's voice. How authentic these accents are let the reader judge.

The Three, who represent the Chief, say to Wilhelm: "One thing there is which no child brings into the world with him; and yet it is on this one thing that all depends for making man in every point a man. If you can discover it yourself, speak it out." Wilhelm thought a little while and then shook his head. After a suitable pause, the Three exclaimed: "Reverence!" Wilhelm seemed to hesitate. "Reverence!" cried the Three a second time. "All want it, perhaps you yourself."

The Three then go on to explain the threefold reverence which they inculcate: reverence for that which is above, reverence for that which is around, reverence for that which is below. The religion which depends on reverence for that which is above is called the Ethnic. The religion which depends upon reverence for that which is around is called the Philosophical. The religion which depends upon reverence for that which is below is called the Christian. This reverence for that which is below is the last step which mankind is fitted and destined to take. Out of these three reverences, conclude the Three, springs the highest reverence of all, reverence for oneself.

To say that Schweitzer's idea of reverence for life came originally from *Wilhelm Meister*—although Schweitzer himself has forgotten the spring from which he drank—is not, however, to depreciate Schweitzer's originality. For Schweitzer has taken that fundamental idea and has developed it into a complete ethical system. There is no indication in *Wilhelm Meister* that Goethe ever carried his idea of reverence to the far point of vision which Schweitzer reaches. With Schweitzer the essential characteristic of reverence is its boundlessness. It includes all that lives, not only that which is above, and that which is around, but the humblest of living creatures, the toad in the posthole, the gnat flying about the lamp, the worm in the road, the flower by the wayside. Goethe thinks of reverence for that which is beneath as reverence for the earth which nourishes us. Schweitzer thinks of it as reverence for the mosquito that stings us, the snake that bites us, the bacterium that kills us. He recognizes the insoluble enigmas which such a view presents, but the reverence he teaches is limitless.

It is of great interest to have Dr. Schweitzer's own comment upon these paragraphs of mine:

I cannot tell exactly the extent and the intensity of Goethe's influence upon me. It is impossible to determine in what he has influenced me and in what he has only confirmed me in the way I was already taking. I believe that the latter rather than the former is the more important. As for the idea of reverence for life, I think I am right in saying that he had no part in the genesis of the idea or of the words. I have always been disturbed by the passage concerning the threefold reverence, because Goethe deals superficially with it instead of going to the bottom of the matter. This passage has always irritated me. The idea of reverence for life came to me as an unexpected discovery, like an illumination coming upon me in the midst of intense thought while I was completely conscious. And when the idea and the words had come to me, it was of Buddha I thought, and not of Goethe. Afterwards I reread the passage about the threefold reverence, but it left me even colder than before. It was still more foreign to me. It did not sound at all like what I had heard within me. This is how it was.

There is another idea that Goethe glossed over without going to the depths of it. It is the idea of the primordial phenomenon [*Urphänomen*]. This also has irritated me. Goethe throws out a word, which may suggest something profound, but he does not reveal it to us. The word is just a sound, enigmatic. . . .

Here, then, are the two men, so much alike in many ways, so profoundly different beneath their likenesses: Goethe brilliant, self-confident, proud, autocratic; Schweitzer simple, humble, lovable, democratic. Goethe the great master of prose and poetry, and the oft-erring but deeply discerning student of life; Schweitzer the great master of music and medicine, and the sublime exemplar of ethical living.

We may ask, again, as many have asked before, why, in one case, all the preoccupation with architects and engineers, with highways and school systems, with forests and finances, while the one incomparable literary talent within him was treated as a lovely but irrelevant thing; and, in the other case, why all the clearing of the jungle and the planting of gardens, why all the building of hospitals and the nursing of the sick, while the sweet harmonies of his spirit and the noble thinking of his mind lay partly dormant and unexpressed? The answer is as simple and as forthright as it is profound. Life itself is the greatest thing! Greater far than its poetry and prose, greater far than its music and its musings. Life itself can be an epic poem or a soul-stirring symphony. To create a life is to create beauty, to plant a garden in a wilderness, an oasis in a desert, a shrine in a city slum. Life is written in deeds, not in words. Its sevenfold seal is its character.

—CHARLES R. JOY

THE ONE HUNDREDTH ANNIVERSARY
MEMORIAL ADDRESS

DELIVERED AT THE CENTENNIAL CELEBRATION

OF GOETHE'S DEATH,

IN HIS NATIVE CITY, FRANKFORT ON THE MAIN,

MARCH 22, 1932

A HUNDRED YEARS AGO TODAY, at nine o'clock in the morning, Goethe raises himself in his armchair, and, believing himself to be on the road to recovery, asks what day it is. When he learns that it is the twenty-second of March he says: "Then the spring has begun, and I shall get better all the sooner."

He does not recall then that the twenty-second of March has long seemed to him a fateful day; he does not remember that unlucky twenty-second of March in the year 1825, when the Weimar Theater, where Schiller had produced in collaboration with him such splendid performances, went up in flames. Delight in the spring sun shining from the skies fills his whole being.

Then his thoughts begin to wander again, but in a moment of regained consciousness he asks that a shutter which has remained closed should be opened, that more light might come in. Before the sun of spring has reached the midday zenith, he has entered into the kingdom of everlasting light.

The city of Frankfort remembers its greatest son on the hundredth anniversary of his death, once more in the brilliant sunshine of spring—but also in the greatest emergency that this city and Goethe's people have ever known.

The spiritual life is threatened by the material life. So much that was being done recently for civilization and for culture must now be discontinued. The hundredth anniversary of the death of Goethe occurs at a moment when the public-school system, which constituted the pride of his people, and to the furtherance of which for over half a century he contributed unstintingly, a school system so peculiarly distinguished, begins to disintegrate.

31

Even the rejoicing which naturally arises among us—because for the first time Frankfort is celebrating a Goethe festival on the property of the university which the sacrificial devotion of its citizens made possible, and upon which, as the city of Goethe, it has a just claim—can hardly find expression. Anxious concern for the future of that university envelops our happiness with gloom. I pray that the good fortune of sister universities which began in the years of deepest necessity and afterwards achieved the most splendid prosperity may be hers also!

May kindly fortune also watch over the ancient and honorable homes of wisdom in Frankfort and keep them safe through all of this trying period!

I hope, moreover, that it may be possible to preserve from ruin the home where Goethe was born, the foundations of which are threatened. The completion of work which is most urgently needed is now rendered uncertain for lack of material.

So pressing are the necessities and the anxieties of this time that the question might arise whether we should not let this day pass by in silence. The answer is found in *Faust*. There the emperor, still suffering from the effects of the turmoil of battle, gives the lord high chancellor permission to hold the festival he requests. The emperor says:

Zwar fühl' ich mich zu ernst, auf Festlichkeit zu sinnen.
Doch sei's. . . .[1]

So let it be.

It is with peculiarly mixed feelings, however, that we do honor to Goethe today. Proudly we remind ourselves of those imperishable and invaluable elements which we find in him and in his works. At the same time we cannot but ask if he has not become a stranger to us, since the age in which

---

[1] My mood is still too stern to contemplate a feast.
Still let it be.

his life and labor fell knew as yet nothing of the needs and problems of our time. Does not the clear light that streams from him shine on to the coming days, which once more will reach the heights where he dwelt, without penetrating into the dark valley where we live?

But away at once with such questions. May that sadness also be banished from this hour which overcomes us when— mindful of the very happy circumstances in which his talents found a peculiarly splendid development—we contemplate those who were unable to bestow upon the world the riches which were theirs because they were snatched away by the war before they were even men, as well as those to whom it is not given to disclose their inner treasure because the destitution in which they live makes it quite impossible.

So great is our grief that we have developed the ability to escape from ourselves, to find inspiration in the knowledge that men once lived their lives under circumstances which permitted them to realize their full manhood, a situation that has become almost incomprehensible to us. Today in such a spirit we approach Goethe, who more than almost any other soul was permitted to live under such favorable circumstances.

Goethe himself fully recognizes how much he is indebted to the circumstances in which his life was passed. Many a time, indeed, he speaks about it—the last time only three weeks before his death, in a conversation with the young Genevese Soret, to whom we owe such valuable sketches of the last ten years of his life.

He is stimulated as he grows up in rich and manifold ways by what he receives from his native city, so hospitable to the social and spiritual life of the time. Once, indeed, he says that he could not imagine another place so favorable, in this sense, for his cradle. Afterwards in Weimar he finds the special preconditions for the spiritual life, as they can only exist at the courts of princes, preconditions which both the great and the little German courts of that time, as seats of the noblest culture, provided in very extraordinary measure. He lives in an age when men were upheld by the spirit of progress then at work. What a ring those passages in *Truth and Poetry* have for us today, in which he informs us that he may be taken as proof that in his youth mutual relations were growing ever better, and thoughts of humanity dominated men! And when he lives through the tremendous upheavals that followed the French Revolution —upheavals which seem to endanger the wholesome development of European manhood—he is able to affirm at last, as he witnesses the end of them, that they were something of transient significance.

He does not come to know material cares. He is spared the fight for existence, for which he is not equipped by nature.

He finds in turn both work and leisure in his place at Weimar in just the measure that each of them is necessary for his development. He is able to serve without ever becoming a vassal; he is able to take part in the government as one who is simply concerned for what is just and useful, without being compelled to waste his strength in coming to terms with parties and party opinions.

At the auspicious moments the people whom he needed in his life enter into it. Herder, Wieland, Lessing, Shakespeare, Spinoza and Jacobi give him whatever they have to give.

In Weimar the prince seeks to anticipate his wishes at every point in friendly understanding, so far as it is possible for him. It is no empty form of words, when Goethe writes on one occasion: "This prince gave me a chance to develop, which would not have been possible under conditions existing anywhere else in my native land."

His friendship with Schiller comes to blossom in 1794

at the very moment when he no longer knows how to escape from the solitude which he has chosen after his return from Italy, and when, lacking the creative impulse, he begins to doubt his poetic talent.

It is indeed true that all those, whether great or small, who help him on his way receive in the end more from him than they give. But he himself, prisoner to those manifold uncertainties and indecisions which are so conspicuously associated with the strength of his will and his creative art, needed those who would bring to him kindness, understanding, encouragement and companionship. That he always found these things from the years of youth to the loneliness of age is the great good fortune that rules his life. Hardly one of the great books that contribute to the perfection of his work would have been possible without inspiration and support in the joy of the task from someone who understood. It was his sister in *Götz von Berlichingen,* his father in *Egmont,* and Schiller in *Faust* and so many other books.

Far be it from us, confronted by such a human personality, to let ourselves go in undiscriminating wonder. There is a great deal in Goethe's life, in his thought, in his work, that we should like to eliminate—very much also that we should like to add to.

Goethe is not an ideal form which directly attracts and inspires. He is less than that and he is more than that.

The fundamental characteristics of his personality are always honesty and sincerity. He may well profess—and he has done so—that lying, hypocrisy and intrigue are as alien to him as vanity, envy and ingratitude.

Around both of these qualities, which determined the course of his life, move other qualities which are not reconciled with one another, but rather spring from the two opposite poles of spontaneity and non-spontaneity. In one moment Goethe is charmingly communicative, and then immediately afterwards he becomes taciturn. He is by nature very kind, but he can in turn be very cool. He takes the most extreme and lively delight in everything he experiences, and immediately afterwards is frankly and anxiously concerned lest he lose his equilibrium. He is impulsive and at the same time indecisive. In his letter of August 27, 1794, to Schiller, he informs his new friend that upon a closer acquaintanceship Schiller will discover a certain moodiness and hesitancy in Goethe which he has never been able to master.

Richly endowed with talent as Goethe also is, he is not by birth either a happy or a harmonious nature, and he has to labor with himself, a labor which is not made easier by the fact that he has many periods of sickness, through which he lost, according to his own testimony, "some of the best years of his life." And how long he was held up by the despondency and inability to work which follow in the train of such illnesses!

Goethe sees that the way he must take is this: not to impose upon himself anything foreign to his nature, but to let whatever good lives and smolders in him develop, and to lay aside whatever is not good in him.

He devotes himself with deepest intensity to this self-discipline. In *Truth and Poetry* he speaks of the inner earnestness with which even in his earlier years he regarded the world and himself. Everyone who comes into touch with him and understands him is impressed by this earnestness.

Disciplining himself in this way, Goethe attains a manhood which is based on truth and sincerity and is distinguished by the absence of envy, by composure, peaceableness and kindliness.

Life offers him rich opportunities to give expression to this lack of envy, this composure and peaceableness. It is simply not true that life is a prosperous and easy existence for him. After the appearance of *Werther* none of his productions receives general approbation. The intimate artistry which is manifest in his later poems alienates people. They had expected, from the writer of *Götz von Berlichingen* and *Werther*, something very different. How many stupid things Goethe had to hear about such a perfect work as *Hermann and Dorothea*, not only from the uncritical masses, but also from those who were intimate with him!

The edition of his collected works which he prepared in Italy has only a very moderate success. His pieces for the stage are hardly played at all. His fame as a poet pales before the ascendancy of Schiller's star. Nobody takes any notice of his researches in the domain of science, for he is not an expert there. Open and covert hostility is active against him.

Quietly and composedly, however, he continues on his way. In a letter to Schelling he ventures to ask the question whether anyone has ever heard him cry out in the midst of all the enmity of which he was the object!

His peaceableness is matched by his kindness. Occasionally, it is true, he is stiff to those who are not so near to him, a stiffness which is taken as coolness and interpreted as pride. This increases with the years as his father's nature comes out ever more clearly in him. At bottom this stiffness —as Chancellor von Müller remarks to Grillparzer, who has been much disappointed in his first visit to Goethe (September 29, 1826)—is only his own embarrassment, caused by his frequent association with little-known or unknown people. On his second visit to Goethe two days later, Grillparzer, in fact, is able to affirm "that Goethe is now just as warm and lovable as recently he was stiff and cold."

True to his deepest nature Goethe is throughout his whole life affectionate and sympathetic. He never withholds himself from anyone who really needs him. This we have from many witnesses. He tries to be especially helpful in every case of spiritual and psychical need that he encounters, for this is most natural to him. Once he asserts that "an imperious habit" forces him to do this. The poem "Aber abseits wer ist's,"[2] which is among the most touching of all that he has written, arose out of this concern for the lonely and the embittered.

Vogel, the physician, who is with him in the last years of his life, informs us that Goethe used to place at his disposal the means of helping the needy whom the doctor encountered in his practice, with something more than the ordinary aid. But he was not permitted to say from whom this generosity came.

So Goethe realizes a human ideal that he has summarized with the words "noble, helpful and good," an ideal whose charm and greatness lie in its splendid integrity and naturalness. As such it affected strongly those who saw it shining from his wonderful eyes; as such it affects us as we see it emerging from his life and his work.

The impression of Goethe's personality must have been great, indeed, for Wieland to describe him as "the greatest, best, most magnificent human being that God has ever created," and for Schiller to say of him that, of all the people he had personally known, Goethe was the man of greatest worth!

As the character of Goethe's human personality is molded by the profoundly natural, so also is the character of his creative being. With Goethe a bit of nature enters into literature. German poetry, and poetry in general, become in his poetry for the first time natural—freed from everything that is unnatural and finding their fulfillment in nature.

It is not by chance that a painter dwells in Goethe with the poet. And if this painter, remarkable as he is, is not allowed to reach the heights, which he tries to conquer in ever renewed attacks, nonetheless he collaborates with the poet in his poetry. Goethe knows how to transplant us with

---

[2] "But who is this man aloof."

magic power into the nature which is there before his eyes and his soul. He has the matchless talent of giving the seen back to us as the experienced.

How wonderful indeed are his similes! He does not invent an image to express a thought; instead of that, pictures of what he has seen and experienced wait within him for the thought which is ordained to take form in them.

Nature is peculiarly dominant in Goethe's writing. In the well-known epigram about the fact that mastery in painting was denied to him, he comforts himself that he has brought his special talent for writing German close to the point of mastery. The mastery consists in this, that the German language comes to its most natural and perfect expression in him. It moves through his poetry with a strength which is primitive and yet, at the same time, refined. It preserves its perfect naturalness not only in form but also in rhythm. It is never dominated by the rhythm of the meters in which it appears, but expresses itself in complete freedom within them and above them.

In accordance with the profound naturalness of his own being, Goethe finds his life bound to nature in an unbroken spiritual union. The boy feels the need of worshiping God at sunrise before an altar on which he has laid an offering of fruit. When the first sorrow hits the fourteen-year-old boy in the unjust suspicion which causes the loss of Gretchen, he seeks comfort in the solitude of nature. He whispers to her, when his remorse over the injustice which he has done to Friederike will not give him rest. She is his confidante. In her he finds himself again.

If the friendship by which men ordinarily encourage one another to do the good, and support one another in misfortune, lies so far in the background of Goethe's poetry, it is because his intimacy with nature is to him the great friendship beside which all other friendship pales.

To separate himself from nature is for him the greatest

mistake into which man can fall. The tragic thought, therefore, which he enshrines in the Faust legend, and symbol-
izes through it, is that of alienation from nature. In the magic
arts to which Faust applies himself—because by the methods
previously tried he has not come close enough to nature to
satisfy his overweening pretensions—he has abandoned nature and thereby has condemned himself to an existence that
must wind up in error and guilt. Awaking after every erring
experience to a new life in nature—these places are among
the most gripping in the poetry of *Faust!*—still he resorts
ever again to the magic spell, until at last there breaks
through in his heart the longing to win again at any price a
natural relationship with nature.

So the key to Goethe's drama of *Faust* lies in the lines:

> Noch hab' ich mich ins Freie nicht gekämpft.
> Könnt' ich Magie von meinem Pfad entfernen,
> Die Zaubersprüche ganz und gar verlernen,
> Stünd' ich, Natur, vor dir, ein Mann allein,
> Da wär's der Mühe wert, ein Mensch zu sein.
> Das war ich sonst, eh' ich's im Düstern suchte. . . .[3]

Up to his last days Goethe lived in a constantly deepening communion with nature. He spends the day before his
last birthday, when he has just finished *Faust* and has
locked it up with a sevenfold seal, with his grandsons in the
splendid late summer weather at Ilmenau, the place where
nature has so often spread her peace over him. For the last
time he reads on the wall of the hunting lodge his "Uber
allen Gipfeln ist Ruh,"[4] which he had written there in
pencil on September 7, 1780. With mind refreshed—so

---

[3] I have not yet fought through to liberty.
If I could from my path all witchcraft banish,
Let all the formulas of magic vanish,
Stood I a man before thee once again,
That would be worth, O Nature, all the pain.
A man I was before I sought the shadows.

[4] "Over all the hilltops is peace."

Chancellor von Müller tells it—as though the peace of the woods and the cool breeze from the mountains had wafted a new breath of life into him, he returns, bearing within him a new appetite for work, which continues until his death.

United to nature in the most intimate fashion, Goethe is creative after the fashion of nature. Therein lies the peculiar greatness of his work; therein lie also its limitations. This is immediately manifest in his creative method. He does not set down in verse the splendor he experiences, but that splendor writes poetry in him. He can work only when the material calls him; when it no longer calls him, he is compelled to let it rest and wait until the call comes again. This way of the cross is the way he goes in his work and at the same time—full of wonder but quite free from envy—he watches Schiller, who is dependent only on his own will, and who can carry on his creative work constantly.

That the kind of natural and creative work for which he is suited sets boundaries and limitations for him he learns also from the fact that he is unable to express himself with equal freedom in every form of poetry. The power, the magic, and the inimitable perfection of his lyric, epic and narrative poems spring from the fact that he is so deeply immersed in nature. The fact that he cannot detach himself from her stands in his way as a dramatic poet. He cannot bring himself to arrange nature and dramatic action for the best stage effects, but insists on letting them appear before the audience as they are found in reality. All of Goethe's pieces, therefore, so far as they are not in themselves suitable for the stage, by virtue of the simplicity of the plot and the simplicity of the nature that appears in them—for instance, *Tasso* and *Iphigenie*—have something that either fails to meet, or surpasses, the requirements of the stage. On the one hand, they scorn current theatrical effects; on the other hand, they make demands on the stage which far exceed its possibilities. Only on the stage of our imagination—for which they are really written—not upon the boards of the theater, can they reach their full effectiveness. However, this does not mean that they do not have their just claim to a place on the boards of the theater.

In his drastic manner, Goethe breaks out on one occasion about the stage conventions to which he cannot become reconciled, in words that are not justified—namely, that one must abandon nature if he turns to the theater, and must be satisfied with "what can be performed for children by puppets in the midst of the laths, pasteboard and canvas of the platform."

One does not seek to correct with clever tricks of stagecraft that which is not suitable for the stage in Goethe and that which surpasses its possibilities, for this only makes more conspicuous the unbridged chasm between stage and reality which is found in him. Only the imagination of the spectator can lift what Goethe wishes to give him, out of the imperfection and incompletion in which it greets him on the stage, to a perfectly comprehended reality.

To what degree Goethe's ties with nature determine the magnitude and limits of his creative work is fully revealed in his material. Hardly ever has any prophecy concerning a poet been so completely fulfilled as the prophecy of Merck, his pitilessly critical friend, who said to the young Goethe that it was his unavoidable destiny to give poetic form to reality.

Indeed it is not granted to Goethe to infuse a material which is outside the range of his nature and his experience with feeling and poetry and so to let it take form in convincing vitality. He achieves perfection—and what a gripping and extraordinary perfection!—only when his work somehow is a revelation of himself. In *Truth and Poetry* he himself states that all of his works are fragments of a great confession. This is not only true of those books, like *Werther, Tasso, Faust, Wilhelm Meister,* in which a central figure appears embodying a bit of his own living soul. The other books also are in themselves a kind of creedal confession, since the very essence of them flows in the last analysis out of his experience. The more one penetrates into the details of Goethe's writings, the more one becomes aware how much of them is in the deepest sense a self-portrayal.

Whenever Goethe, without feeling himself under the moving compulsion of self-revelation, undertakes to treat any kind of theme poetically, something emerges which in spite of this or that excellence bears only vaguely the stamp of his spirit and his talent.

After he has taken over the management of the court theater at Weimar, he feels it to be his duty, as we learn from one of his letters, to write each year a few pieces suitable for the stage. So dubious plays appear like *Der Grosskophta, The Citizen General, The Natural Daughter.* Later Goethe acknowledges that he is unable to carry through this undertaking, and conducts the theater for another half-generation without letting himself be tempted to any further dramatic writing.

The poet Goethe is not, then, a man who can do anything. If youth feels more drawn to Schiller than to Goethe —as it always has felt drawn—this is to be explained not simply by the fact that youth misses enthusiasm in him, but also by the fact that his works do not show the same perfection as Schiller's. It is hard for youth to tolerate the partly successful and the mediocre beside the most sublime.

In reality, every creative spirit must submit to certain laws in defiance of which it cannot progress. Goethe in his masterworks has perfectly fulfilled his mission of sharing with us this rich and noble nature of his, and therewith has made such a precious gift to us that it is unimportant to us to ask how far this gift might have been still further increased by other writings of a different kind.

And the content of this self-revelation? Three mutually related and closely associated motifs run along through it: the growth of nobility, the refining influence of woman, and the consciousness of guilt.

The growth of nobility: Since Goethe recognizes that the way he must travel for himself is a way of self-improvement, never forcing anything upon himself that is foreign to his nature, there do not appear in his books perfect heroes with an ardent realism. Rather it is he himself who appears ever and again in different forms, striving with an incorruptible sense of reality to find, through all his mistakes and failures, the upward way.

All the characters which he draws—we think of those which pass before us in *Wilhelm Meister*—are basically imagined in process of purification, although each of them retains his own nature. This conception of growth in nobility shines forth with soft light in Goethe's simplest sentences, which throughout all time will illumine the way of questing mankind. He, who cherishes as the supreme wish of his life that the ideal of purity may become ever brighter within him, belongs to the pathfinders of humanity.

He consecrates woman as the one who helps to achieve nobility and to guard nobility, because she fulfills this mission in his own life.

Even his first love, Gretchen of Frankfort, takes advantage of the power which she exercises over him, to protect him from those stupidities which would have been beneath his dignity, and to keep him always loyally upright. Later Frau von Stein over a period of ten years is his guide on the way to purity and goodness. After that he receives help in his spiritual development from two princesses at the Weimar court and from other women who are not so conspicuous in the foreground of his life. Out of his life into his poetry these women go, therefore, now in scarcely altered attitude and form, now intermingling in new personalities.

So exalted characters appear, like that of the Princess in *Tasso* and that of Iphigenie. To what heights, in Goethe, the old Iphigenia material rises—through the way in which Iphigenia holds her brother and Pylades back from the path of violence, falsehood and hypocrisy, which they considered permissible for the attainment of freedom, and through the way in which she herself refuses to pay the price of ingratitude to attain it! We remember that in the original Greek version Iphigenia herself points out to the men the way of treachery!

There is hardly anything else in world literature which reaches the level of ethical power achieved in this work of Goethe's, and hardly anything else in which the ethical appears so simply and yet so forcefully.

As profoundly as he experiences the refining influence of women, Goethe also experiences the consciousness of guilt. How the words in *Truth and Poetry* tremble, when later he speaks of the guilt-consciousness into which he has fallen through his behavior to Friederike! When, then, in *Götz*, in *Clavigo*, in *Stella,* and elsewhere, he produces a man who is guilty of imprudence towards a woman and subsequent inconstancy, it is not simply a poetic theme which he has found in his life and out of which he now makes literary capital, but a self-accusation, which will not let him rest.

The tragic guilt of the classics which a man incurs, not through any fault of his own but through inexorable necessity, does not appear in the poetry of Goethe. He sets before us only that which he has experienced, not that which he has imagined. Stark necessity cannot exist for the man who writes: "Our life, like the great whole in which we are contained, is made up in some incomprehensible manner of both freedom and necessity." It is particularly true, as he writes to Zelter in 1830, that he cannot get interested in a case of pure tragedy.

Goethe is well aware that in all the thoughts of guilt and guilt-consciousness with which we are occupied we are touching upon a great secret which we cannot comprehend and cannot fathom. He surmises, however, that the power which guilt seems to have over us is not appointed to destroy us, but in the end must contribute to our purification. Even over guilty men life insists upon its rights. "But man will live" are the words written at the end of the painful lines in *Truth and Poetry* which tell of his consciousness of guilt about Friederike, and then follows: "Therefore I openly took part in other. . . ." To be guilty means to possess a deeper and dearly bought understanding of things.

That earnestness arises from guilt Goethe proves in his own life. When the mature man cannot bear to banish again from his life a woman who has been brought into it through his guilt, but rather gives her a place beside him, accepting all the outer and inner difficulties which ensue for him, it is because the memory of that youthful guilty conscience is still vivid in him, and now points out to him the hard way which he has to go under the much more difficult circumstances of his present guilt. This is one aspect of the Christiane chapter in Goethe's life which is too often overlooked. One man, as we learn from one of his letters, understood Goethe's behavior. That man was Schiller.

How strongly, though all unobtrusively, the thought of purification through guilt, and the thought of sin and reparation in men, which appear in Wilhelm Meister's years of apprenticeship and travel, prove their validity!

When guilt begins to operate in a man he is on the way to salvation through the unfathomable secret of love, which penetrates into the darkness of earth like a beam of eternal light.

Wer immer strebend sich bemüht,
Den können wir erlösen.[5]

Goethe becomes manifestly a thinker in what he reveals about himself as a poet. It is true that all his life long he keeps away from the ranks of the philosophers. In one of his epigrams he proudly boasts that he has been able to get on so well only "because he has never reflected upon thinking." He tries, indeed, to understand Kant, Hegel (towards whom he has a genuine leaning) and Schelling, and endeavors, wherever it is possible, to feel at one with them. But he does not succeed. In the end he is always compelled to reaffirm that they are traveling a road which is not his. He does not comprehend the manner in which the German spirit wages in these thinkers its strife for the ethical, idealistic world view.

Again, it is his profound communion with nature in which both the greatness and the limits of his poetry and thought are fixed. In the last analysis he cannot go along with these thinkers, no matter how much he tries, because their thinking stands between man and nature. Kant's *Critique of Pure Reason* is, therefore, as he says, a prison, which prevents us from enjoying nature in free poetry and thought. Systems of speculative philosophy are also a violation of nature to him.

His inner relationship with nature and his sense of reality do not permit him to treat her in this way. He approaches her with reverence, hoping that she may reveal to him some of her secrets, and may permit him to find that understanding in which strength for life lies. He is striving for a realistic, ethical nature philosophy.

When he writes in *Truth and Poetry*, "A light dawned upon men of lofty thought and spiritual feeling that the direct and first-hand view of nature, and behavior based upon such a view, are the best things that man could desire

---

[5] He who strives onward constantly
Is not beyond our saving.

for himself, and are not at all difficult of attainment," he means thereby the striving for a view of the world and of life to which he himself is devoted.

He will not let his thinking move around in an imaginary and endless circle. The teaching of metaphysics, as it usually goes, is but a vain word-wisdom for him. Only the eternal that appears to him when he submerges himself in nature and in himself has reality and meaning.

> Willst du ins Unendliche schreiten,
> Geh' nur im Endlichen nach allen Seiten,[6]

he declares in one of his utterances.

And how splendid is this other one:

> Was ist Unendlichkeit?
> Wie kannst du dich so quälen?
> Geh' in dich selbst!
> Entbehrst du drin Unendlichkeit in Sein und Sinn
> So ist dir nicht zu helfen.[7]

So he seeks for God not outside nature and coexistent with her, but within her alone. With Spinoza, whom he reveres as his philosophical teacher, he believes in the identity of God and nature. He lives by the conviction that God is in all things, and that all things are in God. He is reassured in this conviction by the saying of Greek wisdom about living and moving and being in God, a saying to which the Apostle Paul refers, according to the Book of Acts, in his speech on the Areopagus at Athens. From his faith in God ring out these lines:

---

[6] Wouldst thou even the endless know now,
Everywhere into the temporal go now.

[7] What is eternity?
Why art thou so tormented?
Enter thyself!
And if in consciousness thou find'st the endless not,
Then is there naught to aid thee.

> Ihm ziemt's, die Welt im Innern zu bewegen,
> Natur in sich, sich in Natur zu hegen,
> So dass, was in ihm lebt und webt und ist,
> Nie seine Kraft, nie seinen Geist vermisst.[8]

Goethe sees the appearance of piety in the fact that man gives spiritual expression in deed to this natural existence in God which he has in common with all being. This he expresses in the moving verses:

> In unsers Busens Reine wogt ein Streben,
> Sich einem Hohen, Reinen, Unbekannten
> Aus Dankbarkeit freiwillig hinzugeben,
> Enträtselnd sich dem ewig Ungenannten,
> Wir heissen's: fromm sein.[9]

Because he knows this one thing, that he belongs to nature and to God, Goethe needs no artistically constructed world view complete to the last detail, but is satisfied to live with a world view which is not complete and cannot be completed. He does not want to be richer than he can be through the absolutely honest acquisition of truth. With that he is confident that he can live.

He characterizes this attitude of his in the words: "To enter into every manifestation of the eternal, so far as it may be explored, to comprehend what may be explored down to its original elements, to reverence unassumingly what may not be explored." He dares to abide by the conviction that "nature is life and progression from some unknown center to some unrecognizable goal," and to rest

---

[8] He rightly is the world's deep-centered motion,
Nature and He in mutual devotion,
So that what lives and moves and is in Him,
Will never find His strength or spirit dim.

[9] Within the pure of heart a yearning surges,
A willing and a grateful resignation
Unto the high, the pure unknown it urges,
Solving the nameless riddle of creation:
We call it piety.

confidently in the assurance "that nothing happens in the life of nature that is not in close harmony with the whole."

In this renunciation of any hope of a perfect world view, Goethe stands alone in his time. His old age falls in the decades when speculative philosophy, because it is confident that it can answer the ultimate questions, dominates the hearts of people and is regarded as the highest and final form of thinking.

How does Goethe, however, introduce ethics into his nature philosophy? The great problem for all nature philosophy—for him as for the Stoics, for Spinoza, for Laotse, the Chinese thinker, with whom Goethe has so very much in common—is indeed how it proceeds from nature to ethics.

Here Goethe takes a very simple path. He does not bother about the derivation and origin of ethics, which the men of his time are attempting to explain, but takes the ethical thoughts which have appeared in mankind as a natural revelation. For, he says, Nature-God reveals itself not only in fundamental physical phenomena, but also in the fundamental phenomena of ethics. The ideas which appear in men are also manifestations of nature, in so far as the history of mankind is a part of the evolution of nature. Therefore, he is firmly convinced that, in a way which we cannot explain to ourselves, the first cause of the world is at the same time the first cause of love, and that this love coming out of the eternal has a concern for us and wishes to find expression in us. So the wind of love blows through the thoughts of Goethe, as it comes out of the prophetical religion of Israel, and out of the religion of Jesus. He who saw even before Nietzsche that the great problem is how man's realization of nobility, which is self-realization, and his achievement of goodness are related to each other— and therein lies his own peculiar philosophical significance! —adopted the simple solution, that true self-realization can consist in nothing other than true realization of goodness. This conception of Goethe's, concerning a nobility which is at the same time a generally accepted goodness, will become influential in the thought of mankind when Nietzsche's rebellion against the traditional notion of goodness which originated in mankind becomes little more than a reminder of the nineteenth century.

And what is the ideal of the perfect human being for the ethical thinker Goethe? A thoroughly simple one. We observe how simple the life of Faust and the life of Wilhelm Meister turn out to be. Faust, who demanded of the world spirit complete knowledge of the world, spends his last days redeeming, from the sea, land which will produce fruit for men. Wilhelm Meister considers it his vocation to place himself at the service of refugees as a surgeon.

What is Goethe's man, of whom so many things have been said so obscurely? He is that for which Goethe strives in his own life: a man of deep sincerity, who at the same time is a man of deed, and as such is a strong but unobtrusive personality.

> Dir selbst sei treu und treu den andern. . . .
> Und dein Streben sei's in Liebe,
> Und dein Leben sei die Tat.[10]

Only that man can understand Goethe who falls under the spell of this deep and simple human ideal of his and is stirred by the spirit of resignation out of which it was born and which makes man fit for life.

This poet and thinker is for us a personality of universal validity, because at the same time he is, very significantly, still practically effective and active in the investigation of nature.

---

[10] To self be true, and true to others. . . .
Let thy search be in affection,
And thy living be thy deed.

Our attention was at first so exclusively directed to the poet that we did not give proper consideration to the meaning of the practical man and the nature student. Only through what the research of the last decades has brought to light concerning Goethe's life and creativity have we become accustomed to see him as he appeared to those who surrounded him in Weimar.

Goethe's governmental activities in the principality of Weimar are not of the kind that people like to suppose— namely, that the poet's court office is just incidental in his life and that he does in it as much or as little as he feels like. He gives himself heart and soul to his job. With what great zeal from the very beginning did he devote himself to bringing order into the finances of the country! Even after his return from Italy, when a part of his work is taken away from him, and he continues to manage only those branches of the administration which have to do with art, science and public instruction, his office still makes great demands upon him. What an impression it makes upon a visitor, who in one of his last years finds him studying the figures of school attendance in all the districts of the arch-duchy of Sachsen-Weimar! Seizing a pen, Goethe at once calculates that school attendance has risen in general and is better in the mountainous regions than it is in the plain!

Natural science also is not just a hobby and a pastime to him, but a vocation. He has spent more time in his scientific work than in his poetry.

So the astonishing fact is that the active and scientific interests are as strong in him as the poetic ones.

Because in this sense he is really universal, we usually honor Goethe as the great posthumous son of the Renaissance. This is not true in every respect. He does, indeed, stand very close to some of the great characters of the Renaissance in his manifold talents, in his kinship with nature, in his yearning for truth, in the independence of his scientific research. At the same time, however, in the absence of enthusiasm, of restlessness, of revolutionary ideas, as everywhere in his whole spiritual being and in the earnestness of his interpretation of life, he is wholly different from them, and much less a man of the Renaissance than Leibnitz perhaps is.

The way, also, in which his manifold talents find expression is very different from the way of the Renaissance men. In the latter these talents burst into flame of themselves, as by spontaneous combustion, and disport and consume themselves in manifold and energetic activity. In Goethe these talents are brought into action, as we learn from himself, by the reflections which arise in him, and by the demands which life makes upon him.

He himself and others as well are aware that he has an eminently practical endowment. Lavater writes in 1774, a whole year before Goethe answers the call to Weimar: "Goethe would be a wonderful actor at the court of a prince; it is there that he belongs. He might have been a king."

And now, at the summit of his first poetic activity, already in the limelight of fame, he faces the question of what he should do with himself in the long pauses that occur, as he already knows from experience, between the periods of artistic creation. So he decides, as he himself says, "to devote himself to world affairs in order that none of his powers should be left unemployed."

The many-sided administrative duties, which for over a decade, from 1775 on, he carries on, involve a responsibility for highway construction, mining, regulation of rivers, and the encouragement of agriculture and forestry. In this work he was led to occupy himself more and more with nature after his scientific interests had found nourishment through his intercourse with doctors from the days of Leipzig and Strassburg on. In the end, then, nature, with which he comes into such close contact, takes complete possession of him. Everything that bears upon it—botany, mineralogy, geology, comparative anatomy, physics, chemistry—interests him.

In his own way—it could not be otherwise with his talents—he arrives at results which contemporary science reaches in another way. He is in advance of this science in many a perception, particularly in the insight—which natural science later verifies—that all forms of life in nature are mutually interdependent, and, in conformity with the law of creation, arise one out of the other.

In his attack, also, upon the view generally accepted at that time that mountains were all of volcanic origin, he is right. We who are not involved in the controversial questions of that day are able to evaluate more justly than his contemporaries the contributions which Goethe made in his scientific writings, and we may say that they were worthy of him.

Goethe is a distinguished observer.

But is it not true that the officeholder and the nature student have unduly suppressed the poet who lives in Goethe, and that so much which only the poet Goethe could create has never therefore been created? It is doubtless true that, if the poet does not rouse himself to finish *Faust* and *Wilhelm Meister* until the closing years of his life, when his hand is already unsteady, the explanation is this, that the officeholder and the nature student have not permitted him to undertake it earlier. Is not this fact, however, that we do not have these two books as the result of a single outpouring, outweighed by this other fact, that they are now two streams in which the experience and thought of Goethe all the way from his youth to his old age are reflected?

Let us not forget that the poet has received at least one great gift from natural science. He is indebted to it for his

friendship with Schiller. Had he not met Schiller, whom
he wished to keep away from because he seemed too much
of a revolutionary, at that memorable session of the Jena
Society for Natural Science, they would never have gotten
together at all. And how many of Goethe's most beautiful
poems would have remained unborn in his soul without this
friendship through which he became a poet once again—
as he himself testifies!

Let us then leave it undecided whether that which the
officeholder accomplished, and the extent, great or little,
to which Goethe contributed to the advancement of natural science, outweigh what he perhaps as a poet neglected
on account of it. It all amounts to just this, that here also
he was himself, and in deep sincerity pursued a course which
he had to take if he were true to his nature. That the great
poet, in his service as an officeholder and in his devoted work
for natural science, stands before us as a man who calls nothing great or small, but does everything that he undertakes
with conscientiousness and devotion, is a living poem, in
itself so moving that it could have been surpassed by no
other that he might have given us in place of it. The most
precious thing about a man, however great his creative activity may be, is always the man himself.

So the peculiar greatness of Goethe's universality consists in the fact that it is the greatness of a well-rounded
and sincere man.

And now finally: What is Goethe's word to us, to us
human beings plunged as we are in terrible need? Has he
a special message for us?

Yes, he has.

All that thought in which a man embraces, not simply
the people of a single age, but humanity itself composed
of individual human beings—and this is true of Goethe's
thought as it is true of hardly any other—has something su-

perior to every age in it. Society is something temporal and ephemeral; man, however, is always man.

So Goethe's message to the men of today is the same as to the men of his time and to the men of all times: "Strive for true humanity! Become yourself a man who is true to his inner nature, a man whose deed is in tune with his character."

But, the question rises, can we still achieve such human personality in the midst of the frightful circumstances of our day? Is the least sign of material and spiritual independence, which the individual must possess if he is to realize this end, to be found among us? The circumstances of our time are indeed such that material independence is hardly known any more by the men of our day, and even their spiritual independence is sorely threatened. All kinds of unnatural conditions are developing daily among us, in such a way that man ceases to feel any longer that he is in every respect a being that belongs to nature and to himself, and becomes more and more a creature submissive to society.

So the question is raised which would have been considered impossible only a few decades ago: Do we still desire to remain faithful to the ideal of human personality even in the midst of hostile circumstances, or are we now on the contrary loyal to a new ideal for humanity which ordains that man shall achieve a differently ordered fulfillment of his nature in the restless merging of his being in organized society?

What, however, can this mean except that we, like Faust, have erred terribly in detaching ourselves from nature and in surrendering ourselves to the unnatural?

After all, what is now taking place in this terrible epoch of ours except a gigantic repetition of the drama of Faust upon the stage of the world? The cottage of Philemon and Baucis burns with a thousand tongues of flame! In deeds of violence and murders a thousandfold, a brutalized humanity plays its cruel game! Mephistopheles leers at us with a thousand grimaces! In a thousand different ways mankind has been persuaded to give up its natural relations with reality, and to seek its welfare in the magic formula of some kind of economic and social witchcraft, by which the possibility of freeing itself from economic and social misery is only still farther removed!

And the tragic meaning of these magic formulas, to whatever kind of economic and social witchcraft they may belong, is always just this, that the individual must give up his own material and spiritual personality and must live only as one of the spiritually restless and materialistic multitude which claims control over him.

That economic relations would some day eventuate in such a destruction of the independence of the individual, Goethe could not foresee. But with that capacity for mysterious foreboding in which he becomes aware of the danger of machinery, the early introduction of which he witnesses, he foresees that the spiritual independence of mankind will be threatened by the appearance of mob rule. This premonition is the basis for his unconquerable aversion to all revolutionaries. The revolutionary is for him the will of the masses bent on overthrowing the will of the individual. Himself a witness of the earliest manifestations of mob rule in the French Revolution and in the wars for freedom, he is profoundly conscious that therewith something appears on the scene the consequences of which will be immeasureable. Hence his hesitant attitude toward the wars for freedom, which was the occasion of so many misunderstandings. He wants freedom for his people, of course, but the manifestation of the mass mind bent on it makes him feel very uneasy, as we learn from a conversation in 1813 with the history professor, Luden of Jena, in the course of which he reveals thoughts filled with profound emotion which at other times he keeps shut up within him.

Goethe is the first who feels something like a concern for man. At a time when others are still unconcerned, it dawns upon him that the great problem in the coming evolution of things will be this: how the individual can assert himself in the face of the multitude.

In this anxious foreboding, which he cherishes within him, and which lies behind many a stormy word which brought upon him the reproach that he was a reactionary and did not understand the signs of the time, there is also concern for his nation. He knows that no other nation so offends against its nature, in the renunciation by its own people of their spiritual independence, as his own nation, this people that he loves with such proud reserve. Yet he knows well that the deep communion with nature, the spirituality, and the need for spiritual independence, which constitute his own being, are manifestations of the soul of his people in him.

And now, a hundred years after his death, it has come to pass, through a calamitous development determined by events and through the influence of that development upon the economic, the social and the spiritual everywhere, that the material and the spiritual independence of the individual, so far as it is not already destroyed, is most seriously threatened. We remember the death of Goethe in this most portentous and fateful hour which has ever struck for mankind. He is summoned as no other poet or thinker to speak to us in this hour. He looks into our time as one most out of place in it, for he has absolutely nothing in common with the spirit in which it lives. But he comes with the most timely counsel, for he has something to say to our time which it is essential that it should hear.

What does he say to it?

He says to it that the frightful drama that is being enacted in it can come to an end only when it sets aside the economic and social magic in which it has trusted, when it forgets the magic formulas with which it deludes itself, when it is resolved to return at any cost to a natural relationship with reality.

To the individual he says: Do not abandon the ideal of personality, even when it runs counter to developing circumstances. Do not give it up for lost, even when it seems no longer tenable in the presence of opportunistic theories which would make the spiritual conform only to the material. Remain men in possession of your own souls! Do not become human things which have offered hospitality to souls which conform to the will of the masses and beat in time with it.

Not everything in history is ordained to be overthrown in the process of constant change, as it seems to superficial observers; on the contrary, ideals that carry within themselves enduring worth will adjust themselves to changing circumstances and grow stronger and deeper in the midst of them. Such an ideal is that of human personality. If it is given up, then the human spirit will be destroyed, which will mean the end of civilization, and even of humanity.

Therefore, it is significant that in this time our eyes should rest on Goethe, the messenger to true and noble humanity, and that his thoughts should spread in every possible way among the people. May his "be yourself" that resounds from them, and contains in this fateful hour for humanity the significance of a historical watchword for the world, make us brave to withstand the spirit of the time and even in the most difficult circumstances to preserve for ourselves and for others as much opportunity as possible for true humanity. And may it be true—for this is the critical thing!—that we, each of us in the measure of his given capacity, may also bring to pass the simple humanity of "let man be noble, kindly, and good," and that this ideal may be among us not simply as thought, but also as power.

Before two decades have come to an end, Frankfort will

celebrate the two hundredth anniversary of the birthday of its greatest son. May it be that he who gives the memorial address at that new festival may be able to state that the deep darkness which surrounds this one has already begun to lighten, that a race with a true feeling for reality is seeking to comprehend it, and is beginning to achieve a mastery over material and social needs, united in its resolve to remain loyal to the one true ideal of human personality.

May the day dawn, then, in which the life of mankind once more flows along harmoniously, naturally, and with renewed vitality, like the music of Bach, with which Goethe was so greatly enchanted because his spirit reappeared in it.

Still, however, we stand under the doom of the words from *Hermann and Dorothea:*

> Denn gelöst sind die Bande der Welt,
> Wer knüpfet sie wieder
> Als allein nur die Not, die höchste,
> Die uns bevorsteht.[11]

So let the other fate rule over us also, and become truth for us, rising from the poem and finding expression in this new poetry:

> Aber es siege der Mut
> In dem gesunden Geschlecht![12]

---

[11] For the bonds of the world are all loosed,
   What ties them together
   But the need, need alone, the highest,
   That now confronts us.

[12] But now let fortitude rule
   In the salubrious race!

GOETHE THE PHILOSOPHER

AN ARTICLE

FROM *Europe*, APRIL 15, 1932:

A SPECIAL NUMBER

DEDICATED TO GOETHE

ON THE ONE HUNDREDTH ANNIVERSARY

OF HIS DEATH

ALL HIS LIFE LONG, GOETHE refused to be a systematic philosopher. In one of his poems he boasts of having achieved splendid results because he never lost his way "thinking about thought."

His dislike of philosophy—so he tells us in *Truth and Poetry*—goes back to his student days. The rationalistic philosophy of the eighteenth century, with which he became acquainted at Leipzig (1765-1768) and at Strassburg (1770-1772), offers him nothing that he does not already know, and irritates him with its doctrinaire quality. He finds fault with it for its scholastic discoloration, especially in its logic and its metaphysics. In *Faust* he expresses freely the feeling that he cherishes.

This philosophy is alien to him also because it pretends to explain everything. By this very fact, he thinks, it proves that it is not giving a true account of the grandeur of nature's mysteries. For example, the materialism advocated by Baron d'Holbach in his *System of Nature*, which appeared in 1770, during Goethe's stay at Strassburg, and which brags of being the quintessence of rationalistic philosophy in giving the simplest explanations of the physical and spiritual world, seems to him to be a dull and decrepit philosophy.

Voltaire, for whom in general he has great respect, displeases him because, in fighting against the narrowness of the prevailing religion, he ridicules the church, the guardian of religious tradition, even while trying to conserve certain fundamental religious truths. For Goethe, the moral and religious tradition preserved in the Bible is something sacred. He knows well enough that not everything in it is of the same religious or ethical value, but he does not want to have pro-

fane hands laid on it. He insists that men should recognize
the existence of mysteries in religion as in nature, and that
men should approach them with respect.

The position taken by Goethe at Strassburg toward the
French and German philosophy of his time remains decisive
throughout his life, as he tells us in *Truth and Poetry*.
Every time he confronts some new philosophy, he studies it
from three principal points of view: (1) Does it touch the
reality of nature without preconceived theories, and does it
bring men into direct contact with nature? (2) Has it a
profound and enlightened ethical idea? (3) Does it have the
courage, when it arrives at the ultimate problems raised by
research and thought, to admit that there are mysteries
that cannot be plumbed, or does it rather presume to offer a
system which explains everything? Every philosophy that
gives a satisfying response to these three fundamental demands he recognizes as plausible.

Whenever he feels that he is dealing with eminent thinkers, he endeavors to penetrate as deeply as possible into their
world of ideas, and he is more likely to exaggerate the inspiration he gets from them than to underestimate it.

He tries hard also not to let himself be dominated by the
distrust which he cherishes instinctively against the philosophers. In a letter to Jacobi, written on November 23,
1801, he defines his position in happy terms:

> To every man, who stands upon his experience, and who is
> and remains always a "philosopher without knowing it" in any
> striking results he may reach, I concede the right to be some-
> how apprehensive about philosophy, and especially about the
> philosophy of our age: but let not his apprehension degenerate
> into aversion: rather let it take the form of calm and prudent
> inclination.

Let us now examine, one after the other, the philosophical
systems with which Goethe came into contact, and the way
in which he reacted to each of them.

Let no one imagine for a moment that Goethe has broken completely with the rationalistic philosophy of the eighteenth century. He sees clearly that the social, economic and intellectual progress that takes place under his eyes is due to the rational, ethical ideal proclaimed by this philosophy. It is only its idea of the world, on which it pretends to base its ideal, that seems to him inadequate.

Basically Goethe recognizes the same end as Kant: to give a safer and deeper foundation to the ethical and spiritual values contained in the contemporary rationalistic philosophy. Kant tries to do this by elaborating a new theory of knowledge, Goethe by examining more profoundly nature itself and the relations of men to it. Kant makes a detour, Goethe goes straight to the point.

To Herder, whom Goethe met for the first time in 1770 at Strassburg, the young Goethe owed very much. He found in him something which he had never before witnessed: a philosopher who had rid himself of all dogmatism, striving to penetrate into reality by the strength of his feeling. Herder revealed to him also certain perceptions concerning the problems of man's spiritual development of which Goethe had had up to that time no idea. Later the two men took divergent roads, for their natures were quite dissimilar, and Herder could not understand how Goethe could hope to comprehend nature by purely scientific labors.

Rousseau enchants Goethe and his Strassburg friends by preaching a return to nature which accords with their own personal ideas. As early as 1791, in his *Metamorphosis of Plants,* Goethe respectfully recalls the "solitary stroller who loved plants," and whose footsteps he had followed in his study of botany.

The Encyclopedists, far from being a healthy influence upon him, plunge him into confusion instead by the very plethora of the things they have assembled.

About Diderot he expresses a curious opinion in *Truth*

and Poetry: "In everything for which the French reproach him he is a typical German."

Upon his return from Strassburg to Frankfort he plunges for the first time into the study of Spinoza (this is in 1774), and discovers in him a masterful teacher who satisfies his deepest aspirations. In the *Metamorphosis of Plants* he declares that Shakespeare, Linnaeus and Spinoza are the three men who have exercised the strongest influence upon him.

The reason why Goethe is so strongly attracted to Spinoza is that he finds in him for the first time ideas clearly formulated which he himself had long felt confusedly and chaotically: that God is not outside nature, but within it and identical with it; that the purpose of ethics is to bring a man to perfection without doing violence to his own nature; that happiness consists in achieving an inner peace. This contact with Spinoza clarifies his own ideas, and purifies his soul. One may well wonder what would have happened to the young Goethe if at the critical moment in his life Spinoza's *Ethics* had not won him to its severe discipline.

Nevertheless, in his memory of Spinoza, reverent and grateful as it is in *Truth and Poetry,* Goethe is fully aware that he has retained his independence. Here is the way he expresses it: "I cannot clearly distinguish between the thoughts which came to me from reading of the *Ethics* and those which I contributed to it." And further on: "Besides, one must not fail to recognize the fact that it is only between opposite natures that the closest ties are really established."

Indeed, it is the Stoic ideas of Spinoza that influence Goethe; the attraction they have for him is so strong that he ignores the rigid, geometrical logic in which they are expressed.

In reality Goethe is a disciple of Spinoza only in so far as he is a Stoic.

His admiration for Spinoza brought him into contact with

Friedrich Heinrich Jacobi, who was one of the first to call attention once more to the thinker then almost forgotten. Goethe went to visit him in Düsseldorf in 1774, and at once felt for him, for the first time, something that he called an intimate friendship. But later, when Jacobi turned away from Spinoza and published his book *Concerning Things Divine* (1811) in which he insisted upon a sharp distinction between pantheism and theism, and postulated the existence of a transcendent and personal God, the friendship of the two men cooled.

In 1784, at Weimar, Goethe took up the *Ethics* of Spinoza again with Frau von Stein. His agreement with Spinoza kept him a bit apart from the philosophic trends of that era.

It is interesting to note the judgment which Schiller, during a brief sojourn at Weimar, pronounced upon Goethe, who was then in Italy, and upon his circle of admirers:

A proud disdain of all speculation, an attachment to nature carried to the point of affectation, a resignation to the fact that one can count only upon the five senses, in short a certain infantile simplicity in the use of reason characterizes him, him and all of his coterie in this place. They prefer to collect plants and study minerals rather than to lose their way in vain, speculative demonstrations. [Letter from Schiller to Körner, August 12, 1787.]

What a splendid mixture of praise and mockery!

Upon his return from Italy in 1788, Goethe has to take a stand in relation to Kant. Reinhold, one of the enthusiastic admirers of the Königsberg philosopher, has won all of Jena to the *Critique of Pure Reason,* which appeared in 1781. "For some time," Wieland writes in a letter of February 18, 1789, "Goethe has been studying Kant's book, the *Critique of Pure Reason,* with great concentration." His conversion to Kant is not, however, very far advanced, when in 1794 he makes the acquaintance of Schiller, and establishes a friendship with him which he has long avoided because of his belief that Schiller is too revolutionary. Schiller, steeped in Kant, bends all his energies to win Goethe to the Königs-berg gospel. It is just to please him that Goethe in all good faith seeks to get rid of what he calls in one place his "im-penitent realism." It is in vain; he always falls back into it. He cannot agree to have no further relations, immediate and frank, with nature. The great formal edifice of the *Critique of Pure Reason* seems to him, as he said in an 1813 discourse in memory of Wieland, "a dungeon which restrains our free and joyous excursions into the field of experience."

Goethe shows great reserve about Kant's discoveries in the domain of the theory of knowledge, but on the other hand acknowledges the everlasting merit of having dis-carded all those ideas which founded morality upon utility, and of having demonstrated the independence and the sov-ereignty of ethics.

He praises Kant also for having sustained in his *Critique of Judgment,* which appeared in 1790, the truth that nature like art is not determined by final causes, and that they are both creative. In this way Kant works with him to raze the restricting walls that hem in the conception of the world elaborated by the rationalism of the eighteenth century, and to restore to nature all of its rights.

But he is unable to pardon the Königsberg thinker for having supported, in his *Religion within the Bounds of Rea-son,* the idea that there is in human nature something funda-mentally evil. He sees in this a concession unworthy of the great thinker to the doctrine of original sin which is so repugnant to him.

This does not prevent him from chanting the praises of Kant when Victor Cousin comes to visit him on October 20, 1817, and from declaring to Eckermann on April 11, 1827, that he considers Kant to be the most eminent of modern philosophers.

He goes so far as to say to the Genevese Soret in 1830: "For in spite of everything, I am also a Kantian." But caution prompts him to add hastily that he only accepts certain affirmations of the Kantian philosophy, and that at other points he holds a very different opinion.

With the representatives of the post-Kantian philosophy he comes into contact through his position as curator of the University of Jena, where the three most important of them taught: Fichte from 1794 to 1799, Schelling from 1798 to 1803, and Hegel from 1801 to 1806.

He has hardly any sympathy for Fichte with his intense nature, and he does not do credit to his real worth; he even regrets that Fichte was called to Jena to succeed Reinhold. When Fichte sends him his great work, *Principles of the Theory of Knowledge,* he replies in a very diplomatic way: "As for me I would be most grateful to you if you would reconcile me to the philosophers that I cannot get along without and with whom I can never come to terms" (June 24, 1794).

His relations with Schelling and Hegel were of an entirely different kind. In both of them he finds again his fundamental, mystical conception that the world is a manifestation of the infinite spirit, and that the soul of the world becomes self-conscious in the human spirit. But this primary idea rests upon an entirely different base with them than with him. With them it comes from logical speculation upon the harmonies of nature and of the infinite; with him it comes from a contemplation which plunges into the mysteries of nature. Tyrannically they force nature to conform to their system: this is what creates a chasm between them that no bridge will ever span. Still he tries to penetrate as far as possible into their thinking.

He separates from Schelling when the latter abandons the idea of the absolute identity of God and nature, as Jacobi had recently done, and places the revelation of God as given by religion on a higher plane than that given by nature.

He has personally great sympathy for Hegel; he appreciates his scientific and historic knowledge. Hegel, for his part, defends Goethe's theories about light and shows great comprehension for Goethe's researches in natural science.

On February 4, 1829, Goethe declares to Eckermann: "Hegel is certainly an eminent man, and the things he says are excellent if one transposes them into his own language."

At a tea given by Goethe on October 18, 1827, in honor of Hegel, who was then staying in Weimar, the guest praises dialectics as the infallible method for discovering truth; to which his host replies by remarking that it also serves to make the false true, and the true false. Then Goethe goes on to praise the study of nature, where one deals with the true infinite and eternal, which no subtlety of logic could change.

Goethe always sees clearly that speculative philosophy, however important and interesting its ideas might be, is untenable, and that it must at last give place to a philosophy of nature which objectively scrutinizes reality. In this expectant attitude, which he alone among his contemporaries holds, he is right.

To summarize: Goethe borrows nothing from any of the philosophies with which he is in contact. Thanks, however, to his conscientious study of the thought of others, he attains an ever clearer grasp of his own ideas.

2. GOETHE'S OWN PHILOSOPHY

Nowhere has Goethe given a general résumé of his conception of the world. But the ideas contained in his works, or scattered through his letters and his conversations, fall into place in a simple and unified philosophy.

Goethe's philosophy is a philosophy of nature based upon an elementary view of reality. The dominant idea of it is this: only that knowledge is true which adds nothing to nature, either by thought or imagination; and which recognizes as valid only what comes from a research that is free from prejudices and preconceptions, from a firm and pure determination to find the truth, from a meditation which goes deeply into the heart of nature.

The knowledge that this research will give us of God, of the world and of man, whether it is great or small, will be sufficient to validate our life. Of this Goethe is persuaded.

If thought in all simplicity and truth sticks closely to nature, it cannot admit that there is any existence outside of nature. It must, therefore, stop thinking of God as a being directing nature from outside. It will not be able to conceive of him except as existing and working within nature. To recognize the identity of God and nature is then, according to Goethe, the point of departure for all subsequent thinking.

Therefore, all things are in God and God is in all things.

Goethe professes this pantheistic mysticism in his poetic writings under forms that are ever new and diverse. At bottom this is nothing but the fundamental conviction which always remains the same in European mysticism, whether ancient, medieval or modern, whenever it passes beyond the obscure stage of feeling and seeks to rise into the sphere of thinking. The mysticism of Goethe has this in common with that of Giordano Bruno (and this is what distinguishes it from that of the Stoics, the medieval mystics and Spinoza): it is allied with the veneration and the vital contemplation of nature. Its distinguishing characteristic is this, that far from ignoring the natural sciences or setting itself above them by some speculative effort, it wishes to be the consequence of them. From that comes its importance and its austere flavor.

The spirit that animates the philosophy of Goethe is revealed in striking fashion in some words spoken to Soret in Goethe's old age: "Nature is always true, always serious, always severe; it is always right and mistakes and errors

are always the work of men. It disdains the incapable, it
gives itself up and reveals its secrets only to that person who
is honest and pure and capable" (February 13, 1829).

Goethe professes this mysticism "of being one with God-
Nature" in a time devoid of all mystic sense. In the eyes of
the rationalist of the eighteenth century, the interrelations
among God, man and the world are as follows: God directs
in the best possible way a world which he has created as the
best possible world, and, on this world stage, man practices
obedience to God. This entirely esoteric idea has its origin
in Christianity. The conception of God which Christianity
has begotten is the result of a historic process which has
raised the ethical God of the people of Israel—the God who
exists outside the world—to the rank of a God who is sover-
eign of the universe. And the great religious problem which
Christianity faces is to know how to harmonize the esoteric
conception of God that results from the contemplation of
nature with the exoteric idea that comes from history, without destroying it in the process.

Christianity, feeling itself threatened by every idea of God
which comes from the contemplation of nature, has instinctively assumed a defensive attitude toward all forms of mysticism and pantheism. That is why it thinks of Stoicism, even
though its ethics are so close to its own, as its mortal enemy.
Therefore, in asserting the identity of God and nature,
Goethe has to resign himself to being regarded as a pagan
by his time.

Of course he can invoke the discourse of the Apostle Paul
to the Athenians. St. Paul, according to the account in the
book of the Acts of the Apostles, cites the verse of the
Greek poet Aratus, who was under the influence of Stoicism:
"In him we live and move and have our being; for we are
also his offspring." In this way he seems to give the mysticism
of "being one with God-Nature" a rightful place in Christianity. In fact, the admirable poems of Goethe about God,

the world, and man make constant allusions to these words
of Stoic mysticism cited in the Acts of the Apostles. However, these words are only an erratic element in New Testament and Christian thought. It is even very problematical
whether Paul actually spoke them at Athens. In his Epistles
we do not find any trace of pantheistic mysticism.

Goethe's thought opens, then, a new phase of the endless
strife in which the naturalistic ideas of God and the Christian ideas of God come to grips.

How does Goethe introduce the element of ethics into his
nature philosophy? The great problem in every philosophy
of nature is, in fact, to pass from nature to ethics. Goethe
proceeds very much more simply than all of the other pan-
theists. The latter—for instance, the classical Stoics and
Lao-tse—affirm, without being able to prove it, that life in
harmony with nature has in itself a moral character; or—as
in the Stoicism of Epictetus and Confucius—they even
clothe nature with a moral character which it does not have
at all. Or indeed they found their ethics, as Spinoza does,
upon considerations which at bottom are alien to their
natural philosophy and which they attach to it afterwards.
Goethe admits simply at the very outset that the ethical fac-
tor is given by nature. Divinity is revealed in nature by
primordial phenomena, which are not only physical but also
ethical (Goethe to Soret, February 13, 1829). Conceptions
which take form in the course of the spiritual development
of humanity are also manifestations of nature to the degree
that the history of humanity is a part of the evolution of
nature. The ethics of love as they are revealed in the thought
of the prophets of Israel and of Jesus, and of humanity in
general, are among these primordial phenomena of the
moral order. Goethe, then, thinks that we know by experience in the deepest and largest sense of this word that God,
who is identical with nature, is, in some mysterious way
quite unfathomable by us, not only creative force but also

moral will. In no other way could the ethical element show itself in the thought of humanity.

So Goethe can concede that we do not encounter any ethical element in nature outside ourselves, and nevertheless insist that the ethical element is a natural phenomenon. The possibility of being noble, good and helpful distinguishes man from all other beings. "For unfeeling in nature," he says in the poem entitled "Das Göttliche":

> Edel sei der Mensch
> Hülfreich und gut!
> Denn das allein
> Unterscheidet ihn
> Von allen Wesen,
> Die wir kennen.
>
> .   .   .   .
>
> Denn unfühlend
> Ist die Natur.[1]

In being moral, man conforms to his own nature. To be in God-Nature means, for Goethe, to be immersed in love.

This is the way in which Goethe solves the problem of problems in philosophy, and reaches a philosophy which is based on nature and still admits the ethical element. It is thus that he reconciles pantheism and Christianity.

The world view which he attains in this manner contains in his judgment all that is necessary for living. As for all the other questions to which his thirst for knowledge would like an answer, he can be satisfied with a presentiment, or

---

[1] Noble let man be,
Helpful and good!
For that alone
Sets him quite apart
From every being
Which we can know.

.   .   .   .   .   .

For unfeeling
Is all nature.

can wait with resignation until such time as they disclose their secret to him.

From that time on his motto will be: "In the domain of the finite, push your research in every direction and grasp the accessible even to the primordial phenomena; as for the inaccessible, venerate it with modesty." That is what he meant when he said to Eckermann: "Man did not come into the world to solve the problem of the universe, but to find out where the problem begins, and consequently to keep himself within the bounds of the accessible" (October 15, 1825).

Having discovered just by the direct contemplation of nature the essential and the indispensable in his idea of the world, Goethe can renounce what is generally understood to be metaphysics. What is usually taught about the supra-sensible world he describes as words without basis or meaning. "God has punished you in giving you metaphysics," he writes to Jacobi on May 8, 1786; "as for me he has blessed me by giving me physics."

"If you would make progress toward the infinite," he says in a fine maxim, "be contented in following all the roads of the finite." And again:

> Was ist Unendlichkeit?
> Wie kannst du dich so quälen?
> Geh' in dich selbst.
> Entbehrst du drin Unendlichkeit in Sein und Sinn
> So ist dir nicht zu helfen.[2]

All that we ought to know and can know about the super-natural is that everything that is natural has a spiritual foundation, that nothing is spiritual alone or material alone,

---

2 What is eternity?
  Why art thou so tormented?
  Enter thyself!
  And if in consciousness thou find'st the endless not,
  Then is there naught to aid thee.

and that there is no mind without matter, nor matter without mind. "The true metaphysics is that which was, is and will be before, at the same time as, and after physics" (*Concerning Sciences in General*).

As for knowing how God, the moral will, is one with God, the creative force—this is also one of the problems for which Goethe claims no solution. It suffices him to know that in some mysterious way, forever eluding investigation, they are one. The earthquake at Lisbon (November 1, 1755), he says in *Truth and Poetry,* upset in him, when he was a six-year-old child, the idea he had had of God as the wise and benevolent governor of the universe. The more he looks with penetrating gaze upon the way of the world, the more he becomes convinced that this God is an enigma. But this does not shake his conviction that there is love in God-Nature. In *Faust* he proclaims that love has its origin in the infinite, and plays its part in human destiny.

But he does not want the natural element in God subordinated to the ethical element, nor does he want dualism reintroduced into the conception of God in any way whatever, under the pretext of explaining everything.

Piety at bottom needs no other knowledge of God than this: We must give ourselves to him. Goethe has explained what he means by piety in gripping verse:

> In unsers Busen Reine wogt ein Streben
> Sich einem Hohen, Reinen, Unbekannten
> Aus Dankbarkeit freiwillig hinzugeben
> Enträtselnd sich dem ewig Ungenannten.
> Wir heissen's: fromm sein.[3]

How moving also is his confession to Boisserée (1815):

---

[3] Within the pure of heart a yearning surges,
A willing and a grateful resignation
Unto the high, the pure unknown it urges,
Unraveling the riddle of creation:
We call it piety.

"There are things of which I can speak to no one except God."

As for the eternal life, Goethe believes that man does not need to know any more about it than what he learns from the identity of God and nature—namely, that every ephemeral being is only a manifestation of an eternal being. If his feeling demands a more perfect representation of what his eternal life will be, he loves to imagine that he will continue to be in some way or other an active being. This is what he means when he says to Eckermann: "The thought of death leaves me completely undisturbed, for I am firmly persuaded that our spirit is absolutely indestructible in its nature, and will be active from eternity to eternity."

We learn how he tries to imagine existence after death by a conversation he had, on the day of Wieland's funeral, with Falk, for whom he had a great esteem because Falk had founded a home for abandoned children. Still greatly moved by the loss of his venerated friend, Goethe unbosoms himself in an unusual way. In picturing eternal existence, he resorts in this interview to Leibnitz' doctrine of monads— although, curiously enough, he never refers to Leibnitz, to whom he is much nearer than to Spinoza. The monads, he explains to Falk, are indestructible, no matter what element or what part of the universe they may belong to. Upon the death of a man, dissolution takes place, in the sense that the principal monad frees from its service the other monads that united with it during its terrestrial existence to form the corporeal being. These monads then return to the elements to which they belong. Then the principal monad becomes once more the center of a new system of monads, a creative force under a new form. Goethe is sure that he has already existed in this way thousands of times, and that he will have to return to the world thousands of times again. But man, he thinks, will not necessarily live again in a human form. Why, he wonders, in this conversation, should I not admit that the indestructible element in Wieland might come to life again in the form of a brilliant star?

What would Leibnitz have said to this way of using his doctrine of the monads?

Goethe, therefore, supposes that "we are not all immortal in the same way" (to Eckermann, September 1, 1829).

It will be noticed that Goethe's idea of the persistence of personality differs from the Hindu doctrine of reincarnation. On the other hand, it is found again in a similar form in certain Chinese thinkers. However, Goethe is always clearly aware that every way of picturing the eternal life is full of contradictions. Moreover, he prefers not to raise the question of "how" in any way. He even goes so far as to declare on one occasion to Eckermann: "To meditate upon our eternal existence is a good occupation for men of fashion and for idle women. But the sensible man lets the world to come rest, and shows himself active and useful in this present world" (February 25, 1824).

What he really thinks about it he has said to Chancellor von Müller, April 29, 1818:

No matter how strongly man may be attracted by the earth and its thousands of diverse phenomena, nonetheless he lifts his searching and nostalgic eyes to the heavens spread out above his head in infinite space, because he feels clearly and profoundly in his heart that he is a citizen of that spiritual realm in which we believe. We cannot help believing in it. We cannot stop believing in it.

In the same way Goethe considers himself excused by his philosophy of nature from every effort to explain that the world means something to man, and that man's ethical life has a meaning for the world. It is here that the fundamental difference between him and all the philosophy of his day resides. In the last analysis, the rationalistic philosophy, as well as Kant and the speculative philosophy, recognizes no other purpose except to give such a meaning to the world that man himself may find a meaning for his own existence. This end forces them to construct complete systems of philosophy which greatly exceed the content of our experiences. Goethe, on the other hand, can content himself with saying: "Nature has no system; she has and is that life force which from some unknown center with one unbroken and continuous effort leads toward an indeterminable goal." He never tires of insisting that in nature nothing is an end in respect to some other end, but that "every creature is an end to itself." In his mind, nature's design, so far as we can speak of a design, is realized to the extent to which each creature achieves fully its own life. "In nature nothing occurs which is not in close relation to the whole." (*Experience as an Intermediary between Object and Subject, 1792.*)

Therefore, man does not need to understand the significance of the universe in order to give meaning to his life and his moral activity. It is by an inner necessity that man must be moral, for this necessity is a part of his being.

Goethe's ethics, therefore, like those of Kant, rest upon a categorical imperative. But the moral activity which springs from an inner necessity is much more simply based for him than it is for Kant.

According to Goethe, becoming moral consists not in a man's introducing moral thoughts into his nature, but rather in providing a continuous effort toward "ennoblement," in the course of which he strives to free himself from the nonmoral elements of his nature and to let all that is good within him achieve its full flowering.

This idea of "ennoblement" dominates all of Goethe's ethics. It is he, not Nietzsche, who is the first to recognize that the great ethical problem is to reconcile the ennoblement of man—that is, the realization of his own nature—with his duty to achieve goodness. He solves the problem by affirming that one never truly realizes himself except through becoming genuinely good. This idea of Goethe's—that the "noble" and the good in the traditional sense of the word merge—will still retain all its vitalizing force in the thinking of humanity when the revolt of Nietzsche against the traditional idea of the good, and his superman, about which there has been so much ado, will be considered as nothing but an episode in the philosophical history of the nineteenth century.

Goethe seeks to achieve this ennoblement in his own person. His greatest desire in life, he confesses, is to achieve an ideal ever more pure and clear. He labors, with the greatest seriousness, to make the sincerity and the nobility that nature has given him the dominant traits of his character. Ceaselessly he tries to realize his motto: "Live in peace with the world." This love of truth, of purity, of peace, is responsible for the grandeur and the serenity of his soul.

In a letter to Schelling, he feels himself justified in affirming that he has never permitted himself to utter the least complaint against all the hostility, overt or secret, of which he has been the object.

One criticism often made of the ethics of Goethe is that it lacks enthusiasm. This is true: the fire of passion seems strangely faint within it; nonetheless a marvelous clarity emanates from it. What is lacking in vitality in his ethics of love is made up for by profundity.

Goethe is an ardent adversary of his contemporary, the English moralist Bentham. The latter in his fanatical utilitarianism insists that every individual should try everywhere and in everything to see that his activity conduces to the greatest possible good for the greatest number of people. Goethe in ill humor characterizes Bentham as an "old fool," and says that by this postulate he does offense to the individual human life and throws disorder into the life of society. "Do not compel me," Goethe says to Soret in 1830, "to take the greatest good to the community as a controlling test for my profoundly personal existence." The greatest good to the greatest number cannot, in Goethe's eyes, be realized by abolishing the natural bonds between the individual and society. The maximum of love and consequently the maximum of well-being will not be attained unless each individual develops within himself, in the most perfect and personal way, the love which nature has put into his heart. In thus taking issue with the utilitarianism of which Bentham is one of the devoted supporters, Goethe reminds us of how Lao-tse rejected the moral utilitarianism of Confucius.

All of Goethe's ethics is contained in these words: "Be true to yourself as to others."

These ethics do not exclude an active love—they imply it. "Let your aspiration be filled with love, and let your life be action," he said in *Wilhelm Meister's Travels.*[4]

All of Goethe's life gave proof of the active love he bore in his heart. He believed his special mission was to sympathize with and to provide for all moral or spiritual distress that he encountered. He was forced to do this, he said at one time, by "a tyrannical habit." He did not withhold his aid from anyone who might have need of it. How beautiful are the words he spoke to Jacobi in 1781: "We should all pity one another."

On December 10, 1781, he wrote to Frau von Stein: "I pray that God will make me each day more economical that I may be generous with all I have, money or goods, life or death." And even before this, on March 12 of the same year, he wrote to her: "I pray the Graces to give me inner kindness and to conserve it in the full measure of my desire."

Vogel, the doctor who cared for Goethe in his old age, tells us that he was able to help a number of sick people with money that Goethe put at his disposal "for people who

---

4 Und dein Streben sei's in Liebe,   Let thy search be in affection
  Und dein Leben sei die Tat.   And thy living be the deed.

needed something more than just alms." But the benefactor
forbade him to disclose his name.

The ethical thinking of Goethe is completely expressed
in the fact that Wilhelm Meister, the character which most
reveals his personality, is moved, by his inner experiences
and by the circumstances of his life, to devote himself to
others and to offer his services as a surgeon to emigrants.

What Goethe, therefore, sets forth as his moral ideal is
the deepening of his inner life, and its expression in moral
action.

Moreover, any true ethics very naturally implies resignation, according to Goethe. In the realization that it is by an
inner necessity that man works to achieve the good, he
should find joy and the courage to be active. He should not
expect happiness from his life or claim to see the result of
his activity. He must not let himself quit when the unreasonable gets the better of the reasonable. "Whoever would
act should resemble the unreasonable sower of the gospel
parable who casts the seed without caring how it will spring
up or where it will spring up" (letter from Goethe to Schiller).

As for himself, this is what he writes to Plessing in 1782:
"All that I can say to you is that even in the midst of happiness I live in a state of constant renunciation, and that
every day with all my troubles and my work I see that it is
not my will that is done, but the will of a higher Power,
whose thoughts are not my thoughts."

Goethe insists strongly upon the ethical character of his
conception of the world and of civilization. The words that
he writes to Eckermann on March 11, 1832, eleven days
before his death, are like his moral testament:

Whatever progress spiritual culture may make, whatever development and deepening the sciences may achieve in an ever
broader search, whatever expansion the human spirit may win

for itself, never will we surpass the grandeur and the moral culture of Christianity, as they shine resplendently in the Gospels.

Such is Goethe's philosophy of nature. It is far from being isolated in history; it is one of the expressions of the simple philosophy of nature, which reappears under ever diverse forms in the European and Chinese thinkers and always leads to a new perfecting of its ethical ideas.

If he had set this forth systematically, it would have probably had some influence over his epoch. It would perhaps have helped to prevent European thought, after the bankruptcy of speculative philosophy, from finding itself so crippled in the face of the natural sciences.

But he enshrined it in his poetry, whence it blossoms for the generations to come in flowers of ever more luminous splendor.

It is to Goethe's philosophy that we may most happily apply what he wrote to Zelter on November 1, 1829, when he was speaking of what a man might bequeath from his experience and his thought to posterity. This is how he expressed it:

If one wants to leave to future generations something from which they may profit, it should be his confessions. He should set himself before them as a personality with his cherished thoughts and his private opinions. His descendants will be able, if they wish, to find there what is good for them or what is part of the eternal truth.

GOETHE AS THINKER AND MAN

AN ADDRESS
GIVEN AT ULM, GERMANY,
JULY 9, 1932

G OETHE IS A THINKER!
Everyone realizes this who has any kind of contact with
him. In every one of his poems some question of world
import is voiced. But this thinker will have nothing to do
with systems of thought, and proudly confesses that he has
been able to go so far only because he has never reflected
upon thinking itself. It can also be said that he has a certain
dislike for what people call philosophy.

How did he come to this point of view? In those very
places where he became acquainted with the philosophy and
thought of the Enlightenment, in Leipzig and then in Strassburg, he felt a certain distrust and coolness towards them.
He noticed that everything he learned from this philosophy
up at the universities he had in reality known of himself.
The thing which was repellent to him in this philosophy of
the eighteenth century was that its conception of the ethical
was not made clear, and that it continually tried in some
almost superficial way to explain the ethical and the good as
the useful. The thought of the eighteenth century was also
uncongenial to him in that it tried to account for everything, and no mysteries remain. In this way it proved that
it had no deeper conceptions of the nature of the ethical.

Goethe's emancipation from the thought of the Enlighten-

NOTE: It will be seen at once that this address follows the outline of
the preceding study from *Europe;* yet there is much new material in it.
Dr. Schweitzer has explained that this address represents his mature
thought much more adequately than the *Europe* article, which is really a
preliminary sketch. After writing the article, Dr. Schweitzer devoted
much time to a further study of Goethe's relations to the philosophers
and philosophy of his age, a matter which greatly interested him. The
Ulm address was the result of these studies.

ment became complete in Strassburg, the break coming
through Voltaire himself. It displeased Goethe to have Voltaire in his thinking make fun of so many things in the Bible
in order to attack the church. Of course, Goethe himself
knew that spirituality and ethics are not always present in
the Christian writings to the same degree of clarity and profundity, but the books of the New Testament were sacred
to him as documents of the Christian faith. He could not
bear that men should scoff at them. So we may say that his
opposition to the philosophy of his time was crystallized by
the Enlightenment in France because of its disdain of Christianity. He would, therefore, have nothing to do with this
school of thought as it was taught in the universities. On the
contrary, as he confessed in *Truth and Poetry,* he and his
friends were thrown completely back upon nature. They
wanted to see how far they could get with nature.

Whenever Goethe in this period of great philosophical
development came into some kind of contact with a philosophical system, he put three questions to it. And his attitude
toward it was determined by the way in which this or that
system of thought answered the questions. The first question
is this: How far is it possible for unprejudiced thought to
approach nature through some kind of system and to bring
man into direct and harmonious contact with it? The second
question is this: How far has this system of thought arrived
at an ethical concept? The third question is this: How far
has this system of thought, if it has advanced to ultimate
problems, come to the point of admitting that it is in the
presence of mysteries from which it can never completely
lift the veils? By the reaction of a certain system of thought
to these three principal questions, was he inclined or disin-
clined toward it. He tried as best he could to understand and
sympathize with it. At times he even forced himself to do
this. For he felt that, when he had to do with the great, his
natural disinclination toward philosophy should not com-

pletely dominate him. In a letter to Zelter he once said on
this point: "The natural dislike which every man who begins
with empirical knowledge has for philosophical thinking
should not degenerate into lasting abhorrence, but" (his
words are quite lovely) "must take the form of a wise and
quiet preference for thought."

What, then, were his relations to the thinkers and the
thought with which he had to do in his narrower life? The
first thinker that exercised an influence over him was Herder, whom he met in Strassburg in the year 1770. In Herder,
Goethe became acquainted with a man who had freed himself from the excessive rationalism of the eighteenth century
and believed that we must enter into the deepest sympathy
with nature in order to understand her. Herder, with his real
intellectual gifts and understanding of history, was chiefly
concerned with the problems of man's spiritual and linguistic
development, and disclosed horizons to Goethe that he had
not suspected. Goethe was enormously grateful to him.

Back in Frankfort again after his stay in Strassburg, he
found his real master in Spinoza. Spinoza was the great,
lonely thinker, who dared to think that God and nature are
mutually interpenetrating, not standing in juxtaposition to
each other. In his principal work, *Ethics,* Spinoza tried by
reflection upon God and nature together to understand the
fact of goodness. What drew Goethe to Spinoza? It was
that he now found clearly expressed in Spinoza the thoughts
that he had himself cherished—namely, that God and nature
belong together, that God works in nature and reveals himself in it. He was further attracted to Spinoza by these words
spoken by the latter: "Ethics consists in this, that a man
achieves for himself the perfection to which he is destined."
No considerations, then, of utility, like those found in the
philosophy of the eighteenth century! "Happiness is an inner
thing." So Goethe was turned back to himself by Spinoza.
He understood himself: the all too stormy nature was qui-

eted. And one may well ask what would have happened
to the young Goethe, in that decisive time after his return
from Strassburg, if Spinoza's profound spirit had not taken
him into its stern school.

And now, full of Spinoza's thought, he was not much
interested in the philosophical currents of his time. To this,
Schiller bore witness. In 1787, while Goethe was in Italy,
Schiller came to Weimar, and in a letter to Körner described
Goethe and his friends. He said:

> Goethe and his school do not like to spend much time with
> philosophy. An attachment to nature carried to the point of af-
> fectation is characteristic of them. A certain childlike artlessness
> in judgment distinguishes him and his friends. They prefer to
> hunt for minerals rather than concern themselves with philo-
> sophical speculations.

But only a year afterwards, upon Goethe's return from
Italy, he had to take up the study of philosophy itself. For
the philosophy of Kant was being taught at the University
of Jena by the distinguished Professor Reinhold. The *Critique of Pure Reason* had just appeared. The fundamental
thought in Kant's philosophy is this: We do not see things
as they are, and things as they really are are unknowable
to us. We must not take reality as reality, for all things
are only appearances in space and time.

Goethe tormented himself now in the endeavor to understand this teaching. We learn from a letter to Wieland in
February, 1789, that he was studying the great work of
Kant with intense application. Then, in 1794, when he became friendly with Schiller, he was compelled by this friendship to study Kant anew. Schiller himself was so immersed
in Kant that he almost lost sight of his own work, and,
because of his love for Schiller, Goethe tried to assent to
this theory of knowledge. He was not, however, successful.
He always came back to his naturalistic realism, which
saw the things around him as real, and accepted things as

they were. In the memorial address on Wieland, which he gave in 1813, he spoke forth: To him and to Wieland this great work, the *Critique of Pure Reason,* seemed like a stronghold which kept people from penetrating freely into the heart of nature. But he found something in Kant that endeared Kant to him: namely, his famous teaching of the categorical imperative. Kant did not endeavor to base the good simply upon the useful. The good is something much deeper than that. He believed that we must subjugate the evil that is in us. Kant was now for Goethe an ally against the superficial conception of the good.

We know that after Kant's day German philosophy underwent a remarkable transformation. There followed a succession of philosophers with fantastic ideas. It is difficult to understand the thought processes of these philosophers, whose heralds say that, when we come to understand how pure being, uniform being, by logical necessity expands into manifold being, then we shall understand the meaning of the world, and in the meaning of the world the meaning of human life. These thinkers, who seem so remarkable to us, started therefore from a deep and strong conviction. The greatest of them in this school of speculative thought were Fichte, Schelling and Hegel; and Goethe was interested in all three of them. And now Goethe was forced by inner compulsion to take a stand in opposition to this whole school of thought, for his watchword was a free and intimate intercourse with nature. Here, however, a kind of strange thought stood between nature and man, the consequence of which attracted him: "The eternal has expressed itself in this mighty and manifold nature."

In some way the great spiritual power of this mystical thought stirred Goethe. He was at one with it, and ignored the fact that he had arrived at this thought through simple communion with nature, whereas the others had come to it through artificially constructed systems. He had no inner

sympathy for Fichte, but he felt drawn in friendship to
Schelling, who was really a great thinker. Particularly did
Hegel attract him. Hegel's great erudition, his extensive
historical and scientific knowledge, impressed Goethe, and
because of this he was ready to forgive him for the very
dull style that he employed. On one occasion he said:
"Hegel is, you know, a very significant man, and he has
much to say that is excellent, if one only translates it into
his own language." But Goethe felt that this whole manner
of philosophical reflection rested on no natural basis. And,
while all those around him believed that in this system of
logical thought the world had arrived at an understanding
never before attained, he knew that it was only a passing
phase. Some day thought would have to come to terms with
nature in a very simple fashion. In this he was right. For
after two decades—in 1848, approximately—this system of
thought broke up.

In this way Goethe analyzed every system of thought that
he encountered during his long life. He took nothing from
any of them, but he studied almost all of them conscien-
tiously and tried through each strange school of thought
to clarify his own thinking.

We now come to those ideas which constitute Goethe's
world view. He never brought them together in a very systematic fashion. They are scattered through his letters, his
poems, everywhere! But quite naturally they fall into place
within a simple unity. We may say that Goethe's thought is
the purest kind of nature philosophy. We reach the truth,
Goethe says, when we do not add our thoughts to nature,
but approach her without preconceived ideas, immerse ourselves in her, turn an attentive ear to her, to see if we may
learn some of her secrets. And when we live in constant
communion with nature, whether we discover much or little
in her, Goethe knows that whatever we find will throw light
upon our way and enable us to live thoughtfully and spirit-

ually. Goethe is prepared from the beginning for the fact that he will not by this means attain a complete world view, like that of the others with their closed systems, but will have to live in an uncompleted house. With this he is content. He begins with the thought that, where nature is everything, we can attain the deepest knowledge of God only by seeking God in nature and accepting the idea that God is in everything and that everything is in God. Next in natural order is the thought that everything which happens is the expression of the incomprehensible nature of God, who is the first cause of being. And this knowledge of God based on nature, this close relationship of man and all things to God, appear again and again in the poems. The God who does not impel nature from without, but maintains it from within—there is nothing new about this expression. The mysticism of ancient, medieval and modern times has always come to this thought. The only peculiar thing about Goethe is that he sets it forth with special earnestness as natural science based upon a very vital experience with nature.

You are aware of the fact that Goethe was not only a thinker, but also a student of natural science. This is what gives to his whole natural conception of God its great fervor, a fervor much deeper than any thinker of the Renaissance evinced. What this fervor is may become clear to you in some words spoken by the aged Goethe. He says: "Nature is always in earnest. She is always austere. She is always true. The mistakes are always on the human side. Nature hides herself from the incapable, and only to the capable and the true and the pure does she surrender herself and reveal her secrets." These things are characteristic of Goethe's world view: veracity, simplicity, starting with nature, losing oneself in nature.

And now Goethe finds himself with the same question that all nature philosophers confront: namely, how does one get the ethical into this thought of nature—in other words, how can one's relationship with nature be an ethical one? Philosophy is always tormented by this question. Goethe takes a very simple path. He says: "The ethical is to be found in nature herself." It appears in the evolution of the spiritual life. There is not only a natural evolution, he says at one time, but also a spiritual evolution of mankind, which is not something peculiar to itself, but also a movement in the evolution of all nature. As plants change and as animals change, so in the spiritual life things do not remain constant, but evolve according to their natural tendencies. And when in the prophets and in Jesus the idea of ethical love appears, it means that the idea of love is in the first cause of being—that is, that God who sustains all of nature and lives in her, God whom I recognize as creative power, is at the same time the first cause of love. I become convinced through experience, Goethe would say, through the observation of nature, that the good is not some kind of a fancy, but something natural in the spiritual evolution of mankind which goes back to God; that man also evolves in his own way, if he is good. So, in some way, God—the first cause of being—and God's will to love are one, although I cannot explain how the two work together, since I see nothing of love in nature. Love is to be found in nature, says Goethe, although I cannot see it. It has emerged in the spiritual evolution of mankind.

And now that he has conceived of his relationship to nature as an ethical one, he knows that man in his spiritual being belongs to God, that now he must live in God through love, and thereby fulfill his life's destiny. So Goethe says: "I do not need to know more than this." He is content to live in an unfinished house. He says: "All other questions I can leave undecided, if I cannot find the answer to them." Goethe's resignation is based upon this knowledge. This is his ideal: "To explore all aspects of the finite which are discoverable, to pursue what can be apprehended, even to the original phenomena in which God reveals himself, but then to reverence the inapprehensible in all modesty." "We are not here to solve nature's problems, but to see where the problems begin in order that we may find our path in the knowable world."

Goethe, therefore, is freed from the necessity of concerning himself with many problems that we formerly considered important for our world view, and of finding an answer to them. He says: "I do not need to concern myself with the question of the relations between the eternal and the temporal. I know that something eternal is revealed in everything that is temporal." Moreover, Goethe does not need to concern himself with the relations between the spiritual and the material. He says: "In everything that we know, in every material thing, something spiritual is disclosed. For as God and nature belong together, so the material and the spiritual belong together." In the thought that the eternal is there in the temporal, that he does not have to roam about in nature to discover it, Goethe finds an extraordinary peace. You remember he says: "If you want to enter into the infinite, penetrate into all parts of the finite." Again: "What is eternity? Why do you torment yourself so? Know yourself, and if you do not find eternity there in your own nature and purpose, there is nothing that can be done for you." It is the same with his thought about a profound immersion in nature rather than a flight over the surface of it. Only so do we come to the truly spiritual and permanent. Goethe in this search stands alone in his time. He does not have to occupy himself with the question of how the ethical God, who requires of me the good, and the creative God, whose works I see in nature, are related. He simply says: They both belong together. Poor man that I am, I cannot understand this. It is a mystery. But I know that they belong together.

Another problem he can leave undecided: the problem of

eternal life. Goethe cherishes a faith in immortality: everything temporal is for him only a manifestation of the eternal.
He says in a certain conversation: "I live in complete
serenity, for I know that human nature is enduring." But
how it is enduring—that is for him a mystery. He says at this
point that we may reflect upon this matter, but that, when
we try to demonstrate clearly that we are immortal beings,
we are thrown into contradictions that prevent us from
thinking the problem through. What we can know with some
assurance about our eternal existence is this, that we continue to work. If anything at all is certain, it is this, that God
has appointed to every individual a task that does not begin
with this life, and does not end with it, but is rather eternal.
Sometimes we find Goethe trying to set forth clearly the nature of this ceaseless work. Coming home from the burial of
Wieland and moved deeply by the occasion, he tells of how
he tries sometimes to describe the eternal life in accordance
with the ideas of Leibnitz' philosophy. "But," he says, "these
are only vague thoughts, and we cannot picture it." Man's
true belief in immortality does not consist in his present
torment of longing for it. The worthy man, says Goethe,
rather justifies his faith in immortality by his labor in this
world. Thus he purifies himself for the eternal work which
God has assigned to him and to which he wishes to devote
himself. This is in simple outline Goethe's faith in immortality.

And now for the last problem, the problem of a world
view, the problem of the meaning of the world. While
thought, in its desire for a perfect world view, will not be
satisfied with the experience of the knowable, but thinks
up ways of making the invisible, the meaning of the world,
comprehensible—yet we always notice that artificiality begins at the very point where in one way or another we try
to give a meaning to the world. Goethe says: "How can man
find a meaning for the world? He is much too small for that

task." This is Goethe's great resignation. We cannot compre-hend the meaning of the world. We must be satisfied to live in the midst of a deep mystery. But while others say, "I must know the meaning of the world in order to understand the significance of my ethical activity in the world," Goethe says very simply, "Man must be ethical from inner neces-sity." Nothing in the world exists for something else. Every-thing in the world has a meaning for itself. But, says Goethe, the single part always has a vital relation to the whole. In other words nothing happens that does not have some relation to the whole. Therefore, the purpose of the world is fulfilled when every single being fulfills his purpose, and I am free to abandon all thought about the meaning of the world while I simply devote myself to the thought that I must realize the meaning of my own life. And, according to Goethe, the meaning of my life is that I should develop the good that is in me, and subdue the evil that tries to re-tard the good. This is Goethe's great teaching about the eternal.

You are aware that another thinker, Nietzsche, has given a new twist to all this ethical thought of mankind. The core of his system is that man should become himself, untroubled by anything else. Goethe knew this profound truth before Nietzsche, the only difference being that he had thought it out in all peace and quiet. What about this "self-realiza-tion" of man? Goethe says: "Man's self-realization can con-sist in nothing but this, to realize oneself in the truly good." Goethe recognizes, then, that the only valid notion of good is the good emerging from love, an idea handed down in the spiritual history of mankind—whereas Nietzsche rejects this notion. So Goethe's ethics is dominated by the conception of becoming noble. In his utterance, "Noble let man be, helpful and good," he places nobility first, because for him it is the dominant thing. "Let man fulfill the good that is in his personality and thereby become truly himself."

In Goethe's mind the conception of the good is not to be regarded as something that is imposed upon us as an obligation, to which all of us in some way must submit. Rather do we have to realize the good that is a part of our personal being, thus perfecting our personality, not everyone in the same way, but each as an ethical being in his own right. The distinctive thing about Goethe's ethics is that he says: "Ethics is something personal." Here he anticipates Nietzsche, who afterwards brings this personal element into ethics as a new problem. In his own life Goethe tried to realize nobility. As a matter of fact these traits were his by nature: "Sincerity, purity of heart and peacefulness." No one can gainsay this in Goethe. Anyone who steeps himself in Goethe's life is gripped by the way in which he clung to his purpose of developing in his life the sincerity, the purity of heart and the peacefulness which were within him. Never did Goethe react in any way to all the open and hidden hostility which he encountered. In the midst of all these attacks he went his quiet and peaceful way. It was so, also, with his extraordinary purity of heart: he went straight on his way always. We find fault with these ethics in that they do not sufficiently exalt an active love, that they lack enthusiasm. But, although the coals of an active love glow with a dull luster in him, we must still admit that the fires burn more deeply. For behind everything stands Goethe's saying: "Everyone must realize the love that is peculiar to him." He is afraid that man will be told: "You must forget yourself." He says: "Think of the love that is in you, which is in you to be realized. Let it become what it wants to become in you."

This was Goethe's real conviction, and it found expression in his old age in a passionate attack upon the English preacher Bentham. Bentham was defending the thesis that every individual must enlist in the service of the whole in order to bring through his activity the greatest good to the

greatest number of people. Then Goethe came and said:
"What does this old fool mean? If he will not let the individual live as an individual but enlists him only in the service
of the whole, then he destroys the natural relationship between the whole and the individual." So Goethe said:

The greatest measure of love in the world will not be attained
by trying to force the individual to give up his own nature. On
the contrary the greatest measure of love will be attained when
each one realizes the love, the special love, that is within him.
More love will then exist, coming naturally out of the individual,
and along with it more happiness, than if we force the individual
to sacrifice his personality, and only permit him to be something
that is good for the whole.

This was the great battle between Goethe and Bentham.
But human thought does not appear at all, if men do not
think the thought that is in them in complete clarity and
purity.

So we may say that Goethe and Bentham represent the
two poles of ethical thinking. For Goethe was not the great
egoist, as people still say he was. Goethe was stiff, awk-
ward and rather shy. He hid this shyness behind a false pom-
posity. But in his inner nature Goethe remained simple
and sympathetic. Now that we have read almost everything
from the archives and letters, we know his real life, and
we can say that he drew back from no one who really needed
him. He gave much time and money to save people. Even
when he was rewarded with ingratitude, he still went on
his quiet way. Just one instance: We learn from Vogel, his
physician, that Goethe placed money at his disposal. When
Vogel called at a poor home, he was able to furnish help
with Goethe's money, not simply with a few dollars, but
with considerable sums, to any extent which seemed necessary to him. Even on his deathbed, Goethe was concerned
in helping one man or another. That was his nature. So we
say with quiet conviction that, although there were times

when Goethe shocked people with a display of coldness and aloofness, all who knew him more intimately were firmly convinced that the love within him was active and vital. Goethe's ideal man was the man who had intensified his life, and from the depths of his nature practiced the love that was in him to make real.

Resignation is a part of Goethe's world view, and this is the thought as he expresses it: One should not do something and then want to see what the results are. Rather must he do good here because of the necessity that is in him, with no concern for the outcome of it. Beautifully Goethe brings this out on one occasion with reference to a parable of Jesus. Let the true man, the man who has a work to do, be like the man in the parable, who sows the seed about him on every side without bothering to see where and how the seed falls. He casts it from him simply because he has it and must sow it. This is how Goethe understands the meaning of this parable.

Here we have, then, the thought of Goethe, which he never set forth in any kind of unified fashion. He would have had a great deal of influence upon his age if he had overcome his reluctance and had set forth his thought coherently; but he considered it his task to introduce into his poems the way in which the mysteries of the world and the mystery of ennoblement had gripped him, and to leave it there, so that, for generations to come, it should continue to glow and bloom for men in ever more lovely colors. So he fulfilled his destiny. He asked: "What can a man bequeath of his spirit to the world?" And this was his answer:

The only thing that we can leave behind us for the men to come is not systems, but confessions and professions. We can set them forth and say: "This was my purpose, this was my wish, this was my thought." And our successors may take from the confession of faith that we place before them whatever seems good to them, whatever is of lasting truth to them.

Therefore, we can say that, although he left behind him no completed world view, Goethe remained true to himself in giving us simply a profession of faith, a profession of the kind of world view which he revealed in his life and as a weak man tried to realize there. The greatest thing about a thinker will always be that his thought and his life form a unity. This is true of Goethe as it is true of hardly any other man. Therefore, even though Goethe had a certain abhorrence of philosophy, he was nonetheless a great thinker. We may also say a benevolent thinker: no one who comes to Goethe will go away with empty hands, but will always take with him something that is good for his own life.

THE GOETHE PRIZE ADDRESS

DELIVERED AT THE GOETHE HOUSE,

FRANKFORT ON THE MAIN,

ON RECEIVING THE GOETHE PRIZE

FROM THE CITY OF FRANKFORT,

AUGUST 28, 1928

As THE FIRST PRIZE WINNER
to be present at the awarding of the Goethe Prize, I may be
permitted to thank the city of Frankfort for its noble purpose. It wishes by public recognition to honor such contemporary work and thought as seem to be in the spiritual
tradition of Goethe.

You, distinguished gentlemen of the board of trustees,
have selected me as this year's recipient. Your choice has
greatly surprised me and has brought me great happiness.
I am so deeply moved that I do not know how to thank you.
Nor can I express to you, Herr Oberbürgermeister, how
your words spoken on this occasion have stirred me to the
inmost depths of my being. You may be sure that you have
given me in these words great encouragement for all the
work that I may be able to accomplish in the years to come,
so long as strength is granted to me.

You, honored gentlemen of the board of trustees, are
responsible for this astronomical event, that I, a poor little
moon, should come today within the orbit of Goethe's brilliant sun. For this you are accountable in the eyes of the
world. That you may be in some measure, however, exoner-
ated, I may tell you that this poor little star had already
been caught within the gravitational field of Goethe's mighty
sun. And I beg you to let me tell you within the brief com-
nur how I first came into touch with Goethe,
ence with him was. I should like in this
nt, so that everyone whom you
n bear witness to his experience
oethe has meant to his inner

sophy that I first had to define

05

my position in relation to him. When Wilhelm Windelband
and Theobald Ziegler, my revered Strassburg teachers, first
introduced me to the newer philosophy, and I was glowing
with enthusiasm for the great speculative systems, it seemed
to me incomprehensible that Goethe, who had lived under
the mighty influence of a Kant and a Fichte and a Hegel,
should somehow stand coldly aside and let all this pass by,
while he remained loyal to the nature philosophy which he
had learned from the Stoics and from Spinoza, and which
he held as a trust to be developed still farther. This astonishing fidelity to what seemed to be insignificant, while something of great importance passed by, had its effect upon me.
I may say that it probably provided the first and most lasting
incentive for me to come to grips with the newer philosophy
and to think my way through to my own convictions. So it
became clear to me as time went by that there were two co-
existing philosophies.

The purpose of all philosophy is to make us aware as
thinking beings of the intelligent and intimate relationship
with the universe in which we have to stand, and of the way
in which we must behave in the presence of the stimuli that
come from it.

One kind of philosophy is able to bring man and the universe together only by doing violence to nature and the
world and by forcing the world into harmony with man's
thought.

The other, the insignificant nature philosophy, leaves the
world and nature as they are, and compels man to find
himself and assert himself in them as a spiritually and crea-
tively triumphant being. The first philosophy is ingenious,
the second elementary. The first proceeds from one mighty
manifestation of thought to another, as they appear in the
great speculative systems of German philosophy, and we
are carried away with admiration for them. This philosoph
has its day and disappears. The second, the plain and si
nature philosophy, remains. An elementary phil

which first of all tried to find intelligent expression in the Stoics and then perished with them because it failed to achieve an affirmative view of the world and of life, strives always to come into its own. This nature philosophy has come down to us in an imperfect form. It tried once again in Spinoza and in the eighteenth-century rationalism to think through to the affirmation of the world and life. When it was unable to do so, violence took the place of effort. The great speculative philosophy brought forth its systems of compulsion. At that time, when everyone was blinded by a world prostrate before thought, there was one man who was not blinded, who remained loyal to the elementary and humble nature philosophy, aware that it had not been able to think its way through to an affirmative conclusion in that eighteenth century in which he lived, but certain that it would have to do so; and he worked toward that end in the simple way which was his inner nature.

When I myself became aware of this and turned back to this nature philosophy—recognizing that it is our appointed task to bring it to an affirmative position in relation to the world and life, in so simple a fashion that all thoughtful people throughout the world would have to share in this thinking, and therein find peace with the infinite and incentive for creative activity—then I realized that Goethe was the man who had held out at the abandoned post where we were once more mounting guard and beginning to work again.

Meanwhile I had had another encounter with him. Toward the end of my student days I reread almost by chance the description of the *Harzreise* in the winter of 1777. And it impressed me wonderfully that this man whom we regard as an Olympian[1] should have set out in the midst of the

---

[1] Although twice in this paragraph Dr. Schweitzer calls Goethe an Olympian, he does not really consider him so. In conversation he has said that Goethe is not a true Olympian, dwelling like a god apart from men. His stiff manners are really a cloak to hide his shyness, and to keep people away from him.

rains and mists of November to visit a preacher's son who was plunged in deep spiritual distress, in order to bring him some spiritual assistance. Once again the profoundly simple man shone forth to meet me from the Olympian. So I learned to love Goethe, and when it happened that I had to undertake some work in my own life for the sake of some man or other that needed help, I said to myself: "That is your *Harzreise*."

I met Goethe again when it occurred to me, in connection with his work, that he could not conceive of any intellectual employment apart from some associated practical activity; and that the two were not bound together by similar natures and definitions, but were quite different and were held together only through his personality. It struck me that, for this great man among the intellectuals, no task was beneath his dignity. There was no practical activity which he thought others, because of their gifts and training, could do better than he. He was intent upon realizing the unity of his personality in the union of practical work and intellectual activity.

I myself held the post of a minister, when I tried to organize my early work. When at that time I sighed that the errands and manifold responsibilities of this office, which I had accepted out of inner necessity, deprived me of time for my intellectual work, I comforted myself with the knowledge that Goethe, with great plans for intellectual activity in his head, sat over his account books endeavoring to put order into the finances of a little principality, passed on plans for the practical construction of streets and bridges, and exerted himself for years on end to bring back into production some deteriorated mine properties. This union of homely activity with intellectual work was a comfort to me in my own life. And when in the course of my life I was led to embrace a field of service which was far from the natural endowment in which I had proved myself, far from the vocation for which I had prepared, Goethe was the comforter who found the words to help me. While others, even those who best understood me, found fault with my decision to study medicine, for which, they said, I was really not fitted, and while they tormented me with objections, telling me that this was quixotic, I was able to reflect that this adventure would not perhaps have been entirely quixotic to him, the great man—who permits his Wilhelm Meister to become at the last a surgeon, in order that he may be able to serve, although he is completely unprepared for it. And thereupon it struck me as significant for us all that Goethe, in his search to understand the final destiny of man, allows Faust and Wilhelm Meister, the very characters in which he depicts himself, to end their lives in a very humble activity through which they become men, he believes, in the full measure of their capacity.

When, then, I began to prepare myself for this new vocation, I once more encountered Goethe. For my medical career I had to take up natural science, even though as a learner and not as an investigator like him. And how remote the natural sciences were from what I wanted to accomplish intellectually before I plunged into my practical work! Then I remembered that Goethe had left his intellectual work to return once more to the natural sciences. It had almost enraged me that he should have lost himself in the natural sciences at the very moment when he should have been bringing into final shape so much that was stirring within him. Now I was myself compelled to concern myself with the natural sciences, though up to that time I had been doing intellectual work exclusively. This experience deepened my nature, and it became clear to me why Goethe had devoted himself to natural science and remained loyal to it. For everyone engaged in intellectual work, it brings immeasurable gain and enlightenment to confront the facts which hitherto he has produced, facts which must be faced not

because he has imagined them but simply because they *are*.
All thinking is strengthened by the fact that in any given
moment it must find its way through reality and no longer
concern itself with imagined things. And when I felt the
compulsion of this "on-through-reality," I was able to contemplate the man who had been through it all before us.

Once again I met Goethe when my laborious student
years had ended and I went out into the world of medicine.
It was as if I conversed with him in the primeval forest. I
had always supposed that I should go there as a doctor.
In the early years, whenever there was building or similar
material work to be done, I took pains to pass it on to others
who seemed to me fitted for it or engaged for it. Soon I had
to admit that this would not do. Either they did not appear,
or they were not qualified to forward the work. So I accustomed myself to work which was very different from my
medical duties. But the worst came later. In the closing
months of 1925, a great famine endangered my hospital,
and I was forced to lay out a plantation for the hospital so
that in any future period of famine we might be able to keep
our heads in some measure above water. I had to superin-
tend the clearing of the jungle myself. The motley array of
voluntary workers assembled from among those who at-
tended the patients would recognize no authority but that
of the "Old Doctor," as I was called there. So for weeks and
months I stood in the jungle trying to wrest fruitful land from
it, and tormented by unruly workers. Whenever I was in
complete despair, I thought of Goethe, who had imagined
his Faust, in the end, busily regaining land from the sea
where men might live and find nourishment. So Goethe
stood beside me in the gloomy forest as the great smiling
comforter who understood me.

If I needs must mention something else that I owe to
Goethe, it is this—that a deep concern for justice goes with
him everywhere. When, at the turn of the century, theories

began to prevail that whatever had to be done should be
done without regard to the right, without regard to the fate
of those affected by the change, and since I myself did not
know how these theories which influenced us all were to be
met, it was a real experience for me to find everywhere in
Goethe a longing to avoid the sacrifice of the right in doing
what had to be done. Ever and again with deep emotion I
turn over the final pages of *Faust,* which—whether in Europe or in Africa—I always read at Eastertide. There Goethe
tells of the final experience of Faust, his last guilty action,
when he determines to get rid of the hut which stands in his
way by a slight and well-intentioned act of violence, because, as he says, he is tired of justice. But this well-
intentioned act of violence becomes in its execution a
frightful deed of violence, in which people lose their lives,
and the hut goes up in flames. That Goethe should add this
episode at the conclusion of his *Faust,* although it retards
the action, gives us a deep insight into the way in which his
concern for justice and his longing to achieve without hurt-
ing worked within him.

My final and lasting experience with Goethe arose from
the extremely vital way in which Goethe shared in the whole
life of his time, its thought and its activity. The currents of
the age surged through him. That is the thing that impresses
one, not only in the young Goethe and the mature Goethe,
but also in the old Goethe. While the mail coach was still
crawling along the highway, and it seemed that the industrial age was only faintly foreshadowed, for him the
industrial age was already there. He was busy with the
problem that it presented, the replacement of the worker
by the machine. If he is no longer master of his material
in *Wilhelm Meister's Travels,* it is not simply because the
old man no longer has the creative power which was formerly at his command, but because the material has grown
into something immeasurable and intractable, because this

old man is putting into this material his whole experience and his whole concern for the future age, because this old man is endeavoring to become, among the men of his time, one who understands the new age and has grown to be a part of it. This is what deeply impresses one in the aging Goethe.

These were the contacts with Goethe through which I came close to him. He does not inspire one. He brings forth no theories that provoke enthusiasm. What he offers us is always what he himself has experienced in thought and deed, what he has molded into higher forms of reality. We come nearer to him only in experience. Because of an experience that corresponds with his, he ceases to be a stranger and becomes a confidant with whom we feel ourselves united in admiring friendship.

My own fate has been such that I have vitally experienced in the very fiber of my being the fortunes of our age and concern about our humanity. That I may experience these things as a free man, in a time when so many whom we need as free personalities are confined in some narrow calling, that I, like Goethe, may serve as a free man because of a fortunate combination of circumstances—this seems to me a grace that lightens my laborious life. Everything that I can accomplish in my work seems to me only a thankful acknowledgment to fortune for this great favor.

Goethe before us lived through this labor and this anxiety for his time. Circumstances have become more chaotic than even he, with his clear vision, could foresee. Mightier than circumstances must our strength be if we are to become, in the midst of them, men who understand our age, men who are an integral part of it.

Goethe's spirit places a threefold obligation upon us: We must wrestle with circumstances, so that those who are imprisoned by them in their exhausting jobs may nevertheless be able to preserve their spiritual lives. We must wrestle with men, so that, distracted as they constantly are by the external things so prominent in our time, they may find the road to inwardness and remain on it. We must wrestle with ourselves and with everyone else, so that, in an age of confusion and inhumanity, we may remain loyal to the great humane ideals of the eighteenth century, translating them into the thought of our age and attempting to realize them.

This is our task, each in his own life, each in his own calling, in the spirit of the great child of Frankfort, whose birthday we celebrate in his birthplace today. This child of Frankfort does not, I think, move away from us with the passing of the years—but draws closer to us. The more progress we make, the more clearly we recognize Goethe as the man who, in the midst of a profound and comprehensive experience, was concerned for his age and labored for it, as we must do, the man who wished to understand his time and to become a part of it.

All this he accomplished with the abounding gifts that had been laid in his cradle here by fortune. It is for us to act as men who have received only one small pound, but who still want to be found faithful in our stewardship. So may it be!

INDEX

Acts of the Apostles, 48, 72, 73
Africa, 14, 25
Agnosticism, 23
Anthony, St., 13
Aratus, 72
Areopagus, 48
Ariosto, 23
Arthurian legends, 14
Athens, 48, 72

Baucis, 56
Bentham, 80, 81, 98, 99
Bible, 63, 88
Boisserée, 76
Bruno, Giordano, 71
Buddha, 27

Chinese thinkers, 78, 83
Christiane, 46
Christianity, 17, 72-74, 83, 88
Church, the, 63, 88
Citizen General, The, 43
Civilization and Ethics, 20
Clavigo, 45
Concerning Sciences in General, 76
Concerning Things Divine (Jacobi), 67
Confucius, 73, 81
Cousin, Victor, 68
Critique of Judgment (Kant), 68
Critique of Pure Reason (Kant), 47, 67, 68, 90, 91

Darwin, 21
Decay and Restoration of Civilization, The, 20
Dialectics, 70
Diderot, 65
Diogenes, 16
Dualism, 76

Eckermann, 68, 70, 75, 77, 78, 82
Encyclopedists, 65
Enlightenment, 87, 88
"Ennoblement," 79, 80, 100
Enthusiasm, 80
Epictetus, 73
Eschatology, 24
Ethics, 50, 63, 64, 72, 73, 79, 80, 82, 88, 89, 94, 98

Ethics (Spinoza), 66, 67, 89
Experience as an Intermediary between Object and Subject, 79

Falk, 77
Faust, 19, 32, 35, 40, 43, 51, 56, 63, 76, 109-111
Fichte, 69, 91, 92, 106
France, 88
Francis, St., 13
Frankfort, 31, 32, 66, 89, 113
French Revolution, 34, 57
Friederike, 22, 39, 45, 46

God, 67, 69, 71-73, 76, 77, 81, 89, 93, 94
Goethe Prize, 105
Götz von Berlichingen, 35, 37, 45
Grenfell, Wilfred Thomason, 13
Gretchen, 39, 44
Grillparzer, 37
Grosskophta, Der, 43
Guilt, 45, 46

Harzreise, 17, 107, 108
Hegel, 47, 69, 70, 91, 92, 106
Herder, 34, 65, 89
Hermann and Dorothea, 37, 60
Hinduism, 78
Holbach, d', Baron, 63
Holy Roman Empire, 22

Ilmenau, 19, 40
Individual, the, 22, 98, 99
Infinite, the, 69, 95
Iphigenie, 41, 44
Israel, 50, 73
Italy, 37, 52, 67, 90

Jacobi, 34, 64, 67, 69, 75, 81
Jena, 55, 57, 67, 69, 90
Jesus, 17, 24, 50, 73, 94, 100

Kant, 47, 65, 67, 68, 78, 79, 90, 91, 106
Königsberg, 67, 68
Körner, 67, 90

Lambarene, 13
Lao-tse, 50, 73, 81